To John

GW00471188

Peaks And Troughs

or

Never Quite Made It But What The Hell?

from

Margery Mason

A catalogue record of this book is available from the British Library

First Edition: July 2005

ISBN: 1-84375-188-7

To order additional copies of this book please visit:
http://www.upso.co.uk/margerymason

Published by: UPSO Ltd
5 Stirling Road, Castleham Business Park,
St Leonards-on-Sea, East Sussex TN38 9NW United Kingdom
Tel: 01424 853349 Fax: 0870 191 3991
Email: info@upso.co.uk   Web: http://www.upso.co.uk

Peaks And Troughs

or

Never Quite Made It But What The Hell?

A Memoir

by

Margery Mason

UPSO

Chapter 1

I know we're all living longer these days, but for goodness sake – ninety? It can't have happened to me, can it? Seems like it, and Lord alone knows how old I'll be if this ever sees the light of day. Posthumously perhaps? "A bunch of yellowing papers found in a cobweb-strewn trunk offers an intriguing peep into the life of a jobbing actress in the last century. Margery Mason, possibly remembered by the older among us as the indomitable Alice North in the long-running "Peak Practice", or even earlier as the odious Mrs Porter in "A Family At War", seems to have put pen to paper …"

Yes, well I did, finally, and here it is, the "intriguing peep".

Starts in 1913. Well no, I don't remember being born, so say 1916, when I started my education – in a dame school. Shouldn't think many people now living went to one of those. Chambers defines them as "Schools for young children usually kept by a woman". Ours had two women, Miss McGuire, rather fearsome, and her nice young niece, Miss Geraldine, both ardent Catholics. We all went, though some of us weren't that young. Kate 9, Grace 7, Bert 5, and me 3. Two teachers, one room, perhaps a dozen kids, a book or so, a piano, a blackboard, slates and squeaky slate-pencils. Almost Dickensian. My first school memory is of Kate leading me up to Miss McGuire with "Please can Margery come too? We don't like leaving her at home and she can do 'A's and 'B's". I promptly flooded my knickers and shoes but there was no fuss. Miss Geraldine, tutt-tutting gently, tidied me up, revealing the shoes were on the wrong feet, which was more humiliating than the "accident". I wonder why on earth Mum chose that school? She never showed any sign of being religious, and Dad, who was away at World War One, was a fairly vociferous atheist. Perhaps it was felt to be less "common" than a Board School. And then she had us all baptised Catholic! Just the kids, not herself. I suppose they must have got at her, Miss McGuire and the local priest; she was always an easygoing woman, liking to keep everyone happy.

So Dad came back and found he'd got four Catholic kids. When I asked him in later life why he didn't do anything about it he said he thought it didn't matter all that much. They could fill us with all those tales and he could say it was rubbish and we could make up our own minds. Very liberal of him but it didn't work so well for me. I swallowed the whole guilt and terror package, so all my childhood I was scared stiff of going to hell. It was so blooming easy. There's a whole great list of Mortal Sins that can have you burning to a frazzle if you don't get to cancel them quick with a confession. I remember – I must have been about 8 – coming out of confession and thinking, "If only I could be run over now and be killed, I'd be safe". I can still see the curve of the road outside the church.

Of course I'd forget about it lots of the time, rushing about climbing trees

A good little Catholic

and scrumping apples (only a Venial Sin, possibly just two years in purgatory), swimming in Tooting Bec's slimy pool, racing my schoolfriend Mollie on our fairycycles, queuing with my non-school friend, Vera, for the gallery at the Old Vic, but the nuns could always bring me back with a jolt.

These were the nuns at our second school, Our Lady of Lourdes Convent. Not really a convent, there were only two nuns and they lived in a real convent up the hill. The other teachers were mostly young Irish girls, just off the boat. Oh and one fascist woman who kept turning up in odd uniforms and hung a huge Union Jack out during the General Strike. I suppose some of them had qualifications, as we took recognised exams, Junior and Senior Oxford, but no-one in our family ever passed one, so I have to believe we were badly taught, as we were really all quite bright. But I mean – Shakespeare was reading four lines each, round the room. The only interest was to look ahead and see if you might get a rude bit; but then it would be cut, "Then slip I from her (bum) down topples she".

They were hot on the religion though, in class and out. I got signed up into various little cults, Child of Mary and the like, all involving guilt if you didn't observe various little rituals. But why did I swallow all this rubbish? Why was I the only one of the kids who fell for it? Was I stupid? Obstinate? Determined to be different? It certainly didn't take with them like it did with me. They neither rebelled nor conformed, just didn't bother with it. And then in due course they all got married in church and had their kids baptised into the Faith! When Grace got married, I was quite keen to know how she'd got on in confession. (You had to confess before they'd give you a church wedding.) "What did he say when you told him about getting drunk?" "Oh I didn't say anything about that." "What about swearing and rude jokes?" "Good Lord, no!" "What did you confess then?" "Oh, you know, forgetting prayers, missing mass, that sort of thing. He was quite nice actually. Only gave me ten Our Fathers for a penance". "Have you said them?" "Not yet, I've been busy." What a wonderfully sensible attitude! Sadly, I couldn't share it and was still obstinately kneeling by my bed in our shared room. I sound like a right sanctimonious little prig, but to be fair, I was actually rather embarrassed by the whole thing. I knew they thought I was soppy, but I felt if I didn't stick to my guns I'd be letting Jesus down.

Also they used to get at me at school about my duty to bring the rest of the family back into the fold. I thought Kate, Grace and Bert could look after themselves, and strangely enough I wasn't worried about Mum, but Dad was a problem. He'd never been christened so I knew the best he could hope for was limbo. Not all that bad, no hellfire or devils poking you with pitchforks, but pretty dreary all the same, hanging about for eternity. So once, when I found him sitting down alone, I leant over and kissed him on the forehead, spitting a bit, and mumbled the magic words: "I baptise thee in the name of," etc. and he was done. He must have wondered what the hell I was up to, as we weren't much of a kissing family. In fact when he and I met in later life after a few years' break, we didn't know how to go about greeting each other. We just shuffled about a bit, half extending our hands, and then sort of bowed.

Hang on a minute! Isn't this book supposed to be about some "jobbing actress" or other? Could we cut to he chase? All right, but pay attention, because this is the unique bit. This is *theatrical history*, and nobody but me seems to know about it. Listen. In the nineteen tens and twenties there were professional companies taking plays, pukka three-act plays, round the Working Men's Clubs in the East End of London. And it was in one of these, The Nora Clements Company, that, at the age of fourteen, I became a professional actor. As far as I can find out, and I've done a bit of research, there are no records anywhere of these companies. And yet they played for years and years. Even the Clubs' headquarters, an imposing building with portraits of past dignitaries, has no record of them. And yet they paid us; we must have gone through the books. I did a radio talk about our company some years ago and a woman wrote in and said she'd been taken to the plays as a

The ancestral home. Mum, Dad, Grandma and Kate

child and had become a lifelong theatre addict. So they existed, these companies, and ours was run by Mum, or Clem as we called her. We were all in it: Dad, who directed, Mum, Kate, Grace, Bert, me and Grandma. Grandma was great. She was really a very sweet, mild person but she had this wonderful line in battleaxes. I've seen her sweep onstage, throw a basilisk glare around the assembled company, fold her arms over her ample bosom, rap out a line and bring the house down. "Ooh," I thought, "I want to do that!"

Of course it wasn't only family in the company. We couldn't make do with just Dad and Bert for the male parts, we needed a heavy, a juvenile, a low comic and so on. I'm not sure how they were recruited. Certainly there were no such things as auditions, or much insistence on experience or even talent. I think Clem just looked at her next choice of play, cast her eye round her acquaintance for someone of the right sex and approximate age and kidded them into having a go. I remember seeing scripts thrust into people's hands with a cheerful "Come along on Wednesday. There's nothing to it, you'll love it". I suppose some of them got out in a hurry but quite a few stayed in for years. Little old Will Murphy for instance, who joined to play Joxer Daly in "Juno and the Paycock" and became Clem's devoted slave, in the company and out. He ran errands, did odd jobs, collected props, took around the publicity and kept her supplied with gossip and compliments. For parties he was dolled up in a white jacket to hand round drinks and knock back all he wanted as part of the deal.

I suppose having this casual approach to acting is why I've never been able to think of it as anything out of the ordinary. Lovely, of course. Oh yes, the thing I wanted to do above everything, but nothing to get too het up about. So when I finally went pro – because we were only semi-pro, most of us had day jobs – I was staggered to find out how desperately people took it. All those first night cries of "Oh God, why do we do it? I'll have to go to the loo again!" My contribution of "For God's sake, it's only acting!" didn't go down too well so I learned to shut up. But acting has always seemed to me to be pretty everyday stuff. I mean, kids do it all the time, playing mothers and fathers, doctors and nurses, acting away like mad. I suppose it's when you get self-conscious and afraid of making a fool of yourself that the rot sets in.

I'm not sure exactly when Clem started the company, but I know she and Dad were always off acting, three or four times a week, and always on Sundays. By that time it was a sort of sideline, but they had been full-time pros earlier on. They may even have met that way. I know they were in a concert party on the front at Bexhill before I was born, Dad doing dramatic monologues and Mum Marie Lloyd songs. There's a picture of them in their pierrot costumes, and one of Mum in a dress the vicar complained about in the local press because it showed her ankles. There was also a mysterious engraving on glass of Mum being fished out of the water by a man in a boat. The inscription said "The popular entertainer Miss Nora Clements being rescued from drowning by heroic fisherman Fred Norton." I was disillusioned when Clem told me it was a publicity stunt, but I shouldn't have been; she was always a good swimmer.

I don't know how much she paid herself for our shows but my first fee was 7/6, which wasn't bad, and I got a double gin in the interval. That was another surprise when I went out into the world. "Oh Margery, not *during* the show, surely!" I've never caved in on that though. After all a show can be terrific fun, like a party, especially if it's a comedy, and what's a party without a drink?

I wonder how the plays were chosen? We certainly don't seem to have played down to our audience. O'Casey, Kipling, Lonsdale, Wilde, Gerald du Maurier – pretty classy stuff! I daresay choice was influenced, as in the reps I later ran, by the 5 males, 6 females, one-set rule, with the added proviso of a good part for Clem. Of course we did the usual run of melodramas and farces. "Tom, Dick and Harry" for instance, which called for identical male triplets continually mistaken for each other. Our actors varied wildly in height, shape and age, but a set of wigs and beards was confidently felt to make them indistinguishable. (Those beards got Mollie and me our parts in the nativity play, she as Herod, and myself as the innkeeper. I got a laugh.) Funny, I don't remember rehearsing. Of course we did, but where? For how long? I know we worked from cue-scripts, handwritten from a single copy of the play. Who had that job? Perhaps the family did them for the rest of the company as well as for themselves. I've never met cue-scripts since. Later, in rep, it was always French's Acting Editions. I've got a feeling these included production notes as well as the text, but perhaps I'm wrong; perhaps we had to scribble in our own XDLs for "cross down left". (In pencil, of course, because the scripts were due elsewhere next week.) What I do remember is my first appearance on the professional boards, and my surreptitious pat from Grandma after my little scene. We were all lined up, cook, butler, parlour maid, and me in front of the mistress. When asked, "What is your name?" I had to step forward and whisper a terrified, "Tweeny, ma'am." "What did you say?" "TWEENEY, MA'AM!" I got my laugh and my pat from Grandma, and the bug had bitten. From them on my schoolwork went finally to pot. I remember thinking, as one of the nuns was tearing me off a strip, "Who cares? Tonight I'll be acting!"

Kate wasn't so keen. The acting was no problem but she jibbed at what she felt was the squalor of it all. Well the dressing rooms were a bit niffy, a combination of the gents' lav next door, stale beer and Clem's greaserag. This was long before Kleenex and though I suppose you could buy removing cream, Clem made her own from clarified lard, spermaceti and rosewater. After a few weeks the rag smelt of anything but roses. I shared her make-up, making great use of the lake liner for the occasional character part. When I came to buy my own I was surprised to find that liners had points. I thought they came with squashed ends. So anyway, Kate got out, though I think she had the most natural talent of us all. She pined all her life for respectability and I always thought she lost out by it. Though she later became a rather good potter and she was always a great gardener. I suppose I just think it's a terrible waste not to act if you can.

Grace, on the other hand, found the whole thing terrifying. She went on, under protest, for a bit part or so, but the crux came when Dad either coaxed or bullied her into a juvenile lead. (I was furious.) On the first night, almost paralysed with terror, she flung herself on stage, fluffed and gagged her way through a scene then collapsed in tears in the wings. Of course she was shoved back on to finish the play, but she never got the taste for it, though oddly enough in later life she took to draping herself in doorways and singing torch songs. Or even leaning on the piano with a long cigarette holder while Kate played. Bert stayed for a while, doing pageboys, urchins and the like, and I believe he was a jockey in "The Sport of Kings", but eventually he priced himself out of the market by demanding ten bob a show.

I, of course, had no desire for escape, only for better parts. I was convinced, when I left school at 15, that it was time for Clem to move over and give me a chance. Of course I was much too young for the glamorous parts, but all I could see was that she was much too old. She was in her mid-forties by then, and stout, even by the standards of the time. I know we all think we can play down – I've done enough of it myself – but Clem made practically no effort to take the years off. She seemed to play all her parts, with complete confidence and great gusto, as herself; and on the whole she got away with it. There was a lot of good-natured twitting in the family: "Act your age, Clem!" was a common cry, and when she played Trilby, the artists' model, we had great fun with her lover's line, "When I saw her sitting for the altogether, it was like a blow between the eyes!" She rose serenely above it all. "Say what you like, it's me they come to see, they love me". And they did; she was enormously popular, with the audience and the company. I secretly thought her a bit corny and unsubtle but I kept quiet about it. Amiable jeering was okay, but serious criticism was showing off. And anyway, I was known to be violently jealous.

Not that subtlety would have stood much chance in our

venues. Echoing halls with bare wooden floors and rows of benches with holes in the back to hold beer glasses. Two waiters serving drink throughout, taking orders, passing up glasses, getting money, passing back change, all during the show. If things got out of hand there was a chairman sitting up front, with his back to the stage, ready to bang his gavel and call for order. The great challenge was to keep them quiet without him. It wasn't always easy, but I can tell you this, as an actor, it taught you attack. All the clubs had scenery, roughly the same. Four sets of different flats, and when you got the booking you said which lot you wanted. There was the oak panelling for high society, the general utility for kitchen, attic, cave or whatever, the garden with waving tree wings and the palace, with flapping pillars and a fountain on a backcloth. Perhaps this was for panto. We never ordered it but we did get it once – for "Juno and the Paycock." Clem could normally take anything in her stride but she did get a bit upset about that. There was nothing to be done, though. Once the set was up it was up. There was some talk of making an announcement, or even putting in a few lines about "That old picture back there that Joxer got a hold of" but in the end we just ignored it and got on with the show. The audience hadn't come for the scenery. They'd seen it all before and they'd see it all again. They were there for a good night out with their mates, their wives and girlfriends and sometimes their kids. There to watch the action, laugh at the jokes, have a drink, sometimes shout a comment or so and clap like mad at the end. No wonder I thought acting was a lark!

Chapter 2

I wonder why I didn't get on with Mum? She was just the sort of person I should have warmed to, a great one for a laugh, and tender-hearted to a fault – in tears over blind pit ponies, that sort of thing – but we were often at odds. Perhaps we were too much alike? It's true I did go on to run my own companies and hog all the leads, which has a familiar ring. Or maybe I wanted a "mumsie" type and that wasn't her scene. I suspect she found herself sadly miscast as Mother of Four and didn't waste too much time in the rôle. Because we were effectively brought up by Miss Jeffries, "Auntie" Anna or AA, who lived with us for about twenty years. We called her a housekeeper but she was more like a slave. Doing all the laundry with a washboard and copper, God help her! Cleaning the house, cooking all the meals, and looking after four careless uncaring kids. She'd been one of ten herself, two of whom died when the whole brood was put in the same room to get the measles over with.

I don't know how old she was when she came to us but she always seemed the prototype old maid: small, thin, repressed and repressive, with the inevitable response of "Never heard of it" to anything new. Poor woman, I can't bear to think of the lousy life we gave her. She was a terrible cook though. We had a weekly menu, never altered. Sunday: meat and two veg because Dad and Mum were home, Monday: the cold joint, Tuesday: the joint made into stew, with sometimes a dessertspoon of curry powder, Wednesday: her day off, Thursday: lamb chops, Friday: fish,

Saturday: sliced ham (standing order with the grocer). Pudding, every day except Sunday: baked apples. Nasty, wizened things with the core left in. They were rather mysteriously kept in a barrel in the drawing room, under the grand piano.

Drawing room, grand piano, housekeeper – sounds a bit grand, doesn't it? Did we nurse pretensions? I've never thought so, but come to think of it we did move from Hackney to Kew and then on to Norwood (not so posh but a bigger house.) Was our "private education" (£2 a term and even then I had to be called out of line and asked to jog my parents' memory) supposed to make us a cut above? I've just thought, when Dad had to fill in my public library application, in the slot for occupation he put "gentleman"! Also he was always bringing home grandiose household items from auction rooms. The drawing room had life-size oil paintings of semi-nudes, floor to ceiling, and the plinths at the bottom of the rather measly front steps sported two large statues we called "Falstaff and his lady". Weird. Not that we were rich. I suspect Clem was a bad manager because a fairly frequent job of mine, which had to be kept from Dad, was a trip to the pawnshop with her wedding ring. She was a great one for parties, which may have had something to do with it. Saturday teatime was open house to the kids' friends – tinned salmon and Lyons French cream slice. I remember an admiring comment, "I say Bert, can't your sisters eat!" Then, if we weren't doing a Sunday show, everybody would be asked round. Turns had to be done, nearly always the same pieces . Dad's chief one was "The Shooting of Dan Magroo" and Clem would give a song or so and accompany everyone else. Clem, Kate and Bert could all play the piano by ear and as I couldn't I was given lessons. I never got any good though I very much wanted to, and practised regularly, sweeping into the freezing drawing room, bowing graciously and sitting down to plonk through the first movement of the Moonlight Sonata. The second movement defeated me; much too fast.

Back to the Clubs! I don't know how many plays we did in my two years with the company but I know we did two World

Premières, the first one written by Laurence, our second lead. This was called "The Chinese Mandarin" and featured him as a treacherous Oriental in a couple of handsome kimonos he'd somehow acquired. The first night we were impressed to see him with a sunflower yellow face and the corners of his eyes taped up under his wig. So it was very upsetting when there was a shout from the front "Call yourself a Chink! Your hands are like raw beef." He made them up for the next performance and added a set of three-inch nails, which made things tricky for Clem, his reluctant bride. I was a sort of native minion scuttling about with my hands up my sleeves and twittering in a squeaky voice. There's only one of Laurence's lines that I remember but it's a good 'un. "Your lover will die like a lat in a tlap. Such is the Mandalin's levenge".

Emboldened by this trailblazing and the thought of avoiding royalties, Clem too wrote a play, a Wild West melodrama. We knew all about the West of course from the movies, but we didn't really know how Americans spoke because it was pre-talkies. So apart from a sprinkling of "Darn tootin's" and "You betchas" which we'd seen on the subtitles, there was little attempt at vernacular, and we used our own Hackney-cum-Norwood accents. "Hell Morgan's Nell" it was called. Clem was Nell of course, and I had my first juvenile lead as an orphanage girl, come out West to teach school. Nell was a saloon entertainer (chance for a song), mistress of Hell Morgan, a hard drinking gambler with an eye for the ladies (Dad). There were two other saloon floosies, Laurence's wife and Grandma in a red wig, and various gun-toting desperadoes, including a moustachioed lecher newly arrived in town.

Hell, deciding the saloon was no place for an innocent girl, sent me off to his remote log cabin. Nell attacked him in a jealous frenzy and when the other women intervened, a fight ensued with lots of scratching and hair pulling (except for Grandma of course) to cries of encouragement from the front. So then she got her revenge by secretly telling the lecher where I was to be found.

Then she discovered, I'm not sure how, perhaps by one of those letters or lockets that turn up in this sort of thing – that I was none other than her own daughter, abandoned as an infant. So at the end of the act, the stage having been cleared by some device or other, she had a big emotional scene, ranging about the saloon, beating her breast and ending up downstage centre on her knees beseeching God to save her little girl. Dad had tried to tone this down at rehearsals but she was adamant it would go over big. On the first night, just as she sank to her knees with some of the lights going out and Ave Maria coming up on the wind-up gramophone, I, flustered with so many cues, gave the wrong one and brought the curtain down. Stopping only for a baleful glare in my direction she swept through the tabs and did the prayer as a front cloth act. She wasn't at all convinced it was an accident but she wasn't a spiteful woman so she didn't crow when my big scene in the next act got the bird.

Alone in the log cabin, I was surprised by the lecherous villain and in no time at all he was chasing me round the room and demanding I yield to his lust. This went over fine. There was no need for the chairman and his gavel, they were riveted, and when he threw me over the table in a violent embrace there were actual cries of "Shame!" and "Get off her you, dirty bugger!" I really thought I'd arrived as a dramatic actress, but then, as he covered my face with kisses, the cries turned to guffaws and shrieks of delight. Cries of "Order" had no effect, and when he turned me upstage and scrubbed at my face with his hastily snatched off neckerchief there were shouts of advice and encouragement. I finally saw his face, with his greasepaint moustache spread all over it, and knew what mine must look like. Still we ploughed on, though every time he tried to clean me up there was a round of applause. Eventually Nell arrived for the big recognition and reconciliation scene, but things had gone too far and after a brief attack on the villain she clutched me to her breast with, "My little girl, my long lost little girl!" and the merciful curtain came down.

There were no recriminations and in fact it was all fondly remembered and retailed for years.

Then eventually the talkies really got in their stride, and dates started to dwindle. Clem held on as long as she could. She revived "Hobson's Choice", always a favourite, with her and Dad in their original parts. I succeeded to Kate's part of Vicky, she came back out of kindness in a cameo role and Grandma, who must have been seventy by now, was a rather unlikely girlfriend for Willie Mossop (that red wig again) and the curtain finally came down on the Nora Clements Company.

For years, after I'd bluffed and lied my way into rep, I kept quiet about how I'd begun, then later I thought it rather smart and my programme biogs began to feature the seven and six and the double gin. Now I've come to think of it as a unique and not unimportant part of this country's theatrical history, and I'm grateful and rather proud to have had the chance to give working people the chance to see live plays at a time when few of them would have thought of going to the West End theatre, and even if they had, they'd have been in the gods, miles away from the action. And though it's the more bizarre aspects of it I've remembered we did take the job seriously and work hard to give value for money. And it's just possible that some of the shows weren't half bad.

Chapter 3

So then it was 1928 and I was 15 going on 16; time to start earning a living. All the family except Bert, who was doing his apprenticeship as a cameraman, were working in the family's second enterprise, this time headed by Dad. He'd had a connection with the film industry since its start, even, so I was told, owning the first cinema in London, the Hackney Bioscope. It would have shown one-reelers (10 minutes) and in my memory the term "penny gaff" seems associated with it. Perhaps that's what they were called, the first little picture-houses? Anyway, now he was running, and indeed ran until late in the forties, the Impartial Film Report, a subscription weekly which reviewed all the tradeshows as a guide to booking – most cinemas were individually owned at that time. There were many more films then – first and second features, shorts, serials, a lot of the stuff that's been taken over by television, and quota quickies, cheaply made British films so cinemas could show their lawfully required quota. The family not only wrote the reviews but also printed them as well on an evil machine called a Multigraph. This was all done from a small office on the third floor of Oxford House in Oxford Street.

There was a dark secret at the Impartial; we ghost-wrote for a rival booking guide put out by the Cinematograph Exhibitors' Association as part of the service to their members. The CEA only had two reviewers so if there were more than two tradeshows at the same time, as there frequently were, the cry would go up

"They want yours!" and our luckless reviewer would have to settle down and write the same review in different words.

As there was never any reason for anyone to call, the office had a very homely atmosphere. There were no takeaway meals then and Lyons Oxford Corner House, though dead opposite, was expensive, so lunch was cooked on the little open fire. Just chops or sausages, all brought in from home – well, where would you buy a chop on Oxford Street? If an official visitor did happen to call it was all hustled under the desks.

I was taken into the fold for a while to work the Multigraph and review some of the lesser films, B Westerns, six episodes of a serial, "Three Stooges" shorts. I hated the printer but rather fancied myself as a reviewer so it was sad when it was reluctantly decided I was surplus to requirements in the family firm and I found myself earning a living as a Multigraph operator elsewhere. The makers had a sort of labour exchange and they sent me out to firms with new style electric machines which frightened the life out of me. Feeling that if life was going to be this grim in the daytime I'd have to find somewhere to act in the evening, I looked around for an amateur company and lighted on the St Pancras People's Theatre. This was rather good as amateur companies went but was run on strangely prudish lines, rather like Shakespeare at school. "Bum" would certainly have been out. "Good Lord" became "My word", "Ask for the use of the lavatory" "Ask for a drink of water" and whole pages disappeared if there was a suggestion of sex. I'd just been cast as Lydia Languish when the War closed the place down. Then I joined the Taverners, who were more sophisticated and more fun. And rather posher. Some of the smart well-to-do girls looked askance at my grimy nails and one bought me a nailbrush. I might have been more humiliated if she'd been a better actress. We did one-acters in rooms above pubs, precursors of today's myriad professional or semi-pro pub theatres. I enjoyed myself with the Taverners. They were very nice to me and when I won a scholarship to an acting school, which had evacuated itself to Witney in Oxfordshire, they took up a collection to help me out.

This was an odd episode. I'd paid ten shillings I could ill afford to enter for the scholarship, of which the first prize was a year's residential tuition with keep, so when I won the second prize and had to find thirty shillings a week for my keep, it was only the Taverners' generosity that let me take it up. I'd somehow got myself an unfurnished room in Belsize Park by this time. My landlady kept asking when I was going to bring in the rest of my furniture but I finally confessed that a bed, two chairs and a table was all there was, then sold the lot to her for ten quid and made off for Witney.

It was a smaller school than I'd expected. Only six other pupils, all in their early teens, and a few evening pupils from the neighbourhood. The principal was an elderly spinster, rather like Miss McGuire but not so kindly, and her assistant, a younger woman, equally aloof. Mime was featured heavily so we and the local kids did a lot of embarrassing flitting about on the village green, being nymphs and trees and clouds and things, giving us healthy appetites, which was unfortunate as food was minimal. A midday meal at a local restaurant with special small plates (we checked on the other tables) and high tea of which I remember only that there were dandelion and nettle leaves for salad and we divided everything rigorously into sevenths. Some of the other pupils who had pocket money got chips in the evening, and once we all got drunk on cider and hatched a rebellious plot which had faded by the morning.

I soon realised that the first prize of residential scholarship had never been awarded, so I bearded the two women in their lair, where we all believed they ate huge meals washed down with whiskey, and asked who'd won the first prize. They said it had been awarded to a very talented young Australian who had since disappointed them by returning to his native land, and that in any case the first prize had been reserved for a male. I said they hadn't mentioned that when they took my ten bob and if they didn't give me the prize I'd go back to London and expose them. I don't know how I proposed to do that but the threat worked and they stopped demanding my thirty bob. They didn't forgive me though. I had a pretty rough time after that and only lasted five weeks. Then they called me in and said that though I had a certain amount of talent I would never get anywhere because I was uncouth, unpleasant and impossible to work with, and I was herewith expelled. I withdrew with dignity and then collapsed in tears. I can't believe that I was so feeble. I was a grown woman for God's sake!

Ten years later there was a rather satisfying sequel. I was working at Worthing when the name of the Witney assistant came up on the next week's cast list. So I kidded my friends in the company to promote me as "Good old Marge, everybody's friend" and they all played up like mad. "Phyllis sends her love. She says you were sweet to her in Keithley!" "Coming to the pub? Oh do, it's no fun without you!" So over the top I was afraid she'd rumble. She was only there for one play and we never mentioned Witney but the day she left she met me in the corridor and mumbled "Thank you". I suppose for not setting fire to her.

Back in Witney and told to leave the premises, I had no money for my fare back to London, but the parents of one of the local children drove me up and I went back to Belsize Park. My old room, now properly furnished, was already let but I took a little one on the top floor and went to sign on. They weren't having any of that, and I was packed off to work in Stepney Labour Exchange. A few weeks there convinced me that it was time to stop mucking about and set to work at being a proper actress. I had some highly glamourised photos done (they used to paint out the flaws and paint in the eyelashes then) and started answering rep ads in The Stage, listing all the parts I'd played, but ascribing them to various obscure reps. No-one would check up, would they?

One of those 'glamour' photos

Chapter 4

I was at Stepney, dealing with my queue in my usual inefficient fashion, when one of my clients turned out to be little old Will Murphy with a telegram, which had somehow been sent to Clem. I'm not sure she and I were on speaking terms at that time, but she'd obviously realised the importance of it and sent her messenger hotfoot on my trail. It was to offer me juvenile leads in Macclesfield Rep at £2 a week. Leaving my queue to wait or riot as they chose, I rushed to the supervisor and announced my departure. To my surprise she was quite sympathetic and said she was sorry to lose a potentially excellent officer. This being the only accolade I've ever received outside the profession, I still treasure it, though with some mystification, as my queue was always twice as long as anyone else's and often had to be taken over by a brisker colleague before it curled round itself. Still, I was off. And oh the joy, the relief, the excitement!

I'd been rather intimidated by the ads in The Stage: "Quick and accurate study" yes, I could do that, but "Dress well on and off", that was dodgy. Anyway, I crammed everything I owned into a case and begged cast-offs from some of the nice smart Taverners. The follow-up letter from Macclesfield had made clear there'd be no fare or rehearsal money, but I had £8 which I thought might see me through, so I set off on the train, hardly able to keep from telling my fellow passengers all about it. I'd never been further North than Oxford so I was thrilled by the landscape, with really high hills and rushing streams, some of them bright green! (I learned later that was from the local dye works.) And when I got out at Macclesfield there were great big hills almost on the platform! "It's like being on holiday!" I thought. The theatre took a bit of finding, but I eventually ran it to earth – a sort of hall over a large building. It was shut at the moment, but the people downstairs told me to go to the local tallow-chandler's who would know all about it. So that's where I met my first pukka theatrical impresario. Having played a bit part or two with the last rep, he'd decided to set up his own company so he could play all the leads. I didn't know this at the time. I presumed he was just the manager, since he was distinctly crosseyed and had only a front tooth here and there. Anyway he gave me the address of a landlady who agreed to take me for 27/6 a week all-in so I went to bed feeling I was on my way as a pukka pro.

The next day was confusing. The "Theatre" was a bit of a shock, though perhaps more to the rest of the company than to me after the Clubs. It was a hall really, but there was a proper stage with a curtain and adequate lighting. Backstage was just one room with a curtain slung across the middle, and, since there was no water, a couple of basins and a pail for emergencies. "Oh really!" said the character juve, "It's like fit-up!" "Isn't it!" I agreed (What's fit-up?). The company was a lot better than might have been expected. There was one remarkable woman whom I've always remembered with respect, gratitude and affection: Ray Parry. She would have been fifty I suppose, tall, slim and golden-haired. And a first class actress, with a beautiful speaking voice. She had been in the touring company of Anew McMaster, of whom I'd never heard at the time but now know was a legend in Ireland. What she was doing in our company Lord knows, but she made no attempt to pull rank or complain, and treated our employer, whose antics got more and more bizarre as his confidence increased, with amused deference. Travelling with Ray was her beloved sister Dot, a sweet gentle woman with the same tolerantly ironic attitude. Neither of them had married and in the digs there was a picture of Ray's handsome fiancé, killed in the First World War.

There was a director, though I can't remember much about

him except that he was short, amiable and drunk most of the time, which I suppose is why he couldn't afford proper food and lived on savoury ducks, a local delicacy made of oatmeal and offal. I think he only lasted for one show and then Ray took over. This was the first time I'd had to play big parts with only six rehearsals, though that was my secret, my CV having listed half a dozen weekly reps. My first part was Scottish, but no one complained about my phoney accent, and the next week I again got the juve lead. The rest of the company were very pleasant. I suppose we were united in adversity, as at the end of the first week our employer (I'll call him Mr K. because I can't bear to write his name) called us in separately and said we'd done such bad business, we'd have to take cuts. I'd used up the £8 I'd left London with on fare, digs and a hat for the first show, so I was in no position to argue, and I expect the rest of the company were in the same plight because we all stayed on. I was reduced to 37/6 a week, which meant there was five bob left after my digs were paid. After a few weeks I got myself a furnished attic and lived a bit cheaper with food from the market. Wonderful crumbly Cheshire cheese was off ration for some reason. Perhaps this was so early in the war that some things were still in good supply, though I remember leeks were sold by the inch.

Clothes were a real problem. The other women had theatrical skips bursting with stuff they'd acquired over the years. I hadn't quite realised that we were barred from repeating an outfit, so I was hard put to it, shuffling my skirts and tops, draping scarves here and there and – as a final desperate resort – disguising plain dresses with patterns of bias binding. Then a wonderful woman came to my rescue. Ethel, head of dressmaking at the local Co-op, wrote and said I mustn't be offended but she often had lengths of stuff left over that she could run up into something for me. Also, she was sure lots of women had evening dresses they wouldn't be wearing in these austerity times, should she ask around?

Several generous people responded and that was a major problem solved. In fact I had a fan letter from two young girls who said they came to the theatre each week just to see what I would be wearing! Food was still a bit of a headache as I had no taste for savoury ducks and Mr K was adamant that he couldn't afford to restore the cuts. But then came a wonderful windfall; Dad send me £20! We weren't exactly at loggerheads though it was some time since we'd been in contact, but he must have heard somehow that I was in rather dire straits. He saved the gesture from any touch of sentimentality by writing that he'd despaired of my ever marrying so this was in lieu of having to fork out for a wedding. I expect he didn't want me to think he'd gone soft. But what did I care? Twenty quid, it was a fortune! I wrote an ecstatically grateful letter and promised to pay for my own wedding if it ever happened. As I did, ten years later.

Meanwhile, I was having a ball. No waitressing, no shop, no hated Multigraph, no being bullied and sacked – nothing to do but act all these whopping great parts! Even though a lot of them were opposite Mr K. He and I made an interesting King Charles and Nell Gwynne, me with my scalp turned green from the copper dust I'd put on my hair, and he with his gap teeth, and his cross eyes peering out from under an enormous wig.

It was shortly before this production that our troops had been rescued from the Dunkirk beaches, and he conceived the idea of interrupting the play with a patriotic "tabloo" celebrating the event. This involved the whole company scurrying about behind the curtain, lugging boxes into place and mounting them, waving swords, tridents and Union Jacks. Just as the curtains were about to part on this spectacle I saw that he, having flung off his wig in the mêlée, had forgotten to replace it. I didn't tell him. Another time we romped about together in "Honeymoon Beds", I resplendent in satin and lace (good old Ethel), he in striped flannel pyjamas with a hint of woolly vest at the neck. Our major triumph though was in "Trilby" with him as Svengali of the piercing, hypnotic eyes and me in Clem's old part. It wasn't easy to keep them quiet even in the early scenes but the climax came after his death. I had to struggle up from my pallet bed and throw aside the hanging which shrouded his legacy to me, a portrait of himself. This hadn't been produced at the dress rehearsal and I thought I was prepared for the worst, but when the cloth fell and revealed Mr K himself sitting on a kitchen chair and poking his head through the frame, it wasn't only me that corpsed; the audience fell about. I then had to reel around the stage, madly singing my swan song, collapse and fall lifeless to the ground. I embarked on my song, but of course it couldn't be heard, so the prompt corner didn't get a cue to bring down the curtain, and Mr K just sat there raking the audience with his crossedeyed basilisk glare while the delighted roars went on, until Ray, standing by as Lady Castlemaine, came to the rescue. Next day she persuaded him to get a photo doctored up. She could always handle him better than anyone else, perhaps because she had this traditional principle that the employer was boss, however ludicrous. She, Dot and I would giggle at him in private but she was unfailingly courteous to him, however high-handed he became. And he was certainly that, sweeping into rehearsals for the last hour with "Right, now we'll do all my bits." And being very sharp with Harry Shacklock, our most amiable and compliant second lead, because he slopped the bucket on his way to empty it. I had only one real set-to with him and of course I lost it, but as I had to slap his face in the play that week, one almighty wallop ensured he was a bit more polite to me for a while.

It's funny that nobody ever really rebelled. Of course we were all scanning The Stage each week. But it was a difficult time in the theatre (when isn't it though?) with a lot of London theatres dark and jobs in the provinces more attractive than usual, so we were up against stiffer competition than normal. A few actors must have managed to move on because I remember some newcomers. I wonder if Peter Vaughan, now a very successful heavy, remembers his stint in Macclesfield? He arrived a slim blonde seventeen- year-old. Actors had to be under or over recruitment age, or what was rather insultingly called "C3" so we were delighted with this glamorous addition to our number. The audience were pleased too. At his first entrance in full white-tie evening dress (I wonder where he got it?) there was a burst of applause before he even opened his mouth.

All this time Ray had been urging me to write and send photos in all directions, saying it was ridiculous I should be stuck in this place (what about her?). Finally it paid off. A letter from Buxton invited me to phone them. I had a terrible cold and was feeling ghastly as I crawled out to the public phone. After I'd agreed to join the company at four pounds a week as juve lead, I positively bounced back to my digs, every cold symptom gone like snow in summer.

I bade a sad but exuberant farewell to the Perry sisters and Ethel, my benefactress at the Co-op. I now had a fair stock of clothes, but she promised to be on hand if I needed her, and indeed she was for many, many years. That was one of the lovely things about weekly rep; the townspeople really felt you belonged to them. Not in the way of TV viewers who will stop you in the street with "Don't I know you?" (I still like that, though; it's fame of a sort) but with genuine friendliness and even affection

I don't know that the Buxton company was much better than Macclesfield except of course for our leading man, but things were more comfortable backstage and the money seemed a fortune. An unforeseen snag was that although I'd been engaged as juve lead, the boss's daughter quite often fancied what I thought of as my parts. This wasn't too much of a blow though. Character parts can be more interesting than juveniles and I was often happily busy with the lake liner. One week I could have wished I needn't to look glamorous. Over the weekend I had developed a huge abscess under a tooth root and couldn't get any treatment until Monday, when it was yanked out, leaving half my face swollen to enormous proportions, one eye closed and a mass of mauve and yellow bruises. I plastered the make-up on and tried to do most of the play in profile. It was a pity she was supposed to be a femme fatale.

I had a great time at Buxton, walking miles over the dales and swimming in any bit of water that offered itself. Again I thought,

"It's like a holiday!" Thank goodness I've always been a "quick and accurate study" so there was plenty of time to make the most of the country. It was even more like a holiday when Vera and her husband and little girl came to stay. When I waved them off, I was taken aback to find myself quite desolate. I hadn't realised how much I needed friends from my old life as well as new ones.

I next went to Oldham, a step up in money (£6) and in status. I was now a leading lady and started to play all the best parts, and not just in my own age range. There were lots of good parts written for middle-aged women in those days. Edith Evans, Sybil Thorndyke, Marie Tempest, Lillian Braithwaite, I played all the parts they'd created. You could always tell a Marie Tempest part; everyone talked about her for two-thirds of the first act, then she made her entrance.

The standard was better too. Of course weekly rep's weekly rep, but there was a good feeling at Oldham. We took it seriously and did our very best. I'm going to have a bit of a wallow now. A few years ago, having drinks after the private showing of a telly film I'd been in, the producer, whom I hadn't before met, said, "I've never been able to forget your Saint Joan. Whoever plays it I still hear your voice." "I wish it were true," I said quite honestly, "But you must be thinking of somebody else. I've only played it in weekly rep." "Yes," he said, "at Oldham." Of course he'd have been very young and first impressions last, but still!

While I was chucking my weight about in all these parts a young local girl by the name of Dora Broadbent joined the company. She was pretty, but somehow no great shakes in juvenile roles, but my golly when she got a chance at comedy, especially dotty old ladies! She had the same quality as Grandma; she could just come on and bring the comedy with her. So it was no surprise when she later found her niche and became highly successful as Dora Bryan. Then a local schoolboy was hired for just one show. "My God," I said, "That boy knows what he's up to. He gets it right every time. Can't we take him on as an ASM or something?"

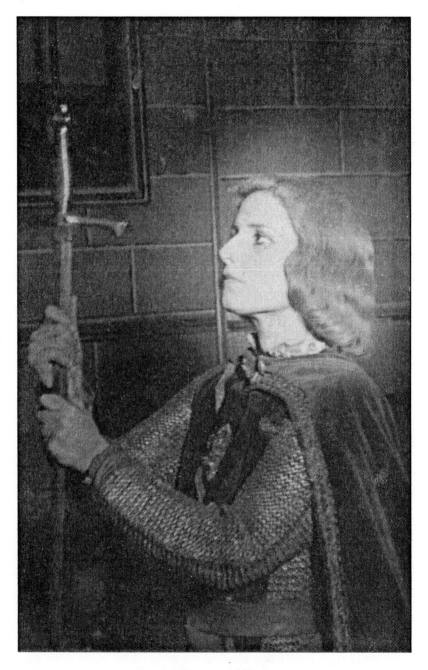

St. Joan at Oldham

"He'd have to lose his accent," they said. "He'll get nowhere talking like that." Howya doing, Bernard Cribbens?

Work was great at Oldham but, oh dear, the town was depressing. Even the moors were so dirty the backside of your pants was black if you sat down. I had digs in Coronation Road with Ada, who'd brought lugubriousness to a fine art. "Had a good day, Ada?" I'd say as she brought my supper in. "Good? I've been that miserable I've cried four times." "Four times – what for?" "Don't ask, just don't ask." She was a spectacularly awful cook too. I was "buying-in" – you buy, she cooks – and I once found a newspaper wrapping still on the fish under the soggy batter. She cried about that too. There was heavy bombing going on in Manchester, so there was nowhere much to escape to. Once there was an art exhibition in the Oldham Library and I rushed along, thirsting for a bit of colour. It was a Lowry retrospective.

It isn't that I don't like the North – and especially its people – and I respect the affection they have for their rather grim towns. I don't know if they still do it, but they used to whiten not only their front steps but also the pavement in front of them. That could teach Swiss Cottage a thing or two. Nevertheless I pined for more greenery than the blackened privet round the Library, and perhaps for somewhere in the South where I could get an occasional glimpse of London. So I wrote to Harry Hanson, king of the Court Players, a dozen or so weekly reps, some of them twice-nightly. Harry was a legend in the rep world, mainly for his assorted wigs and undisguised camperie. I went to tea with him at the Queen's Hotel in Leeds and fixed a job in Worthing at £8 a week. "But Margery," he said, "Don't get too ambitious. I can tell you, it's lonely on the heights."

You couldn't get at the sea in Worthing for barbed wire but there were sunken gardens on the front and parks and clean air. Gorgeous. There were also German fighters flying over and machine-gunning, but not often. It was at Worthing that I first noticed that when old couples – and there were a lot of them – are out shopping it's always the man who threads his hand through his wife's arm, to be towed along in her wake. She's the leader now. Actors are supposed to take note of things like that and store them away for reference. I don't think you ever do so consciously but when you come to feel your way into a part, they sort of happen to you.

Again the company was friendly, with quite a bit of talent and a great asset in a good-looking leading man of the right age, a conscientious objector who had somehow managed to get himself transferred from farm work to acting. He was also a vegetarian and a Buddhist and a bit of a womaniser. But very nice, and good to work with. He came to a very sad and awful end. He was accidentally killed in a train, his head knocked off in a tunnel. A few years later I was in the Salisbury in St Martin's Lane, which used to be an actors' pub and maybe still is. I was drinking with a group when someone mentioned George's end. "How exactly did it happen?" I asked. "He was leaning out of the window." "Oh," I said, "Throwing up, I suppose. He was a bit of a boozer." "Really?" said a woman rather frostily. "Did you know him?" "Oh yes," I said, "Did you?" "Quite well. I was married to him." I slunk off to the loo and out by another door.

Clothes were becoming a problem again. They were strictly rationed and although actors got an extra page of coupons, Harry Hanson's fondness for "Anyone for tennis?" type plays sometimes meant five or six changes a night. Furnishing fabric was off ration so curtain lace dyed black made a negligée or velveteen a ball gown. Then urgent calls would go out to other companies – "Can I borrow the pink peignoir?" "Any of your lot got a maid's outfit?" And there was always Ethel, faithful as ever.

I was a Court Player on and off for ten years. Ten years in weekly rep! It's supposed to ruin an actor. Easy options, mannerisms, tricks, shallow characterisations – all these are supposed to be the inevitable result of churning out a new performance week after week. Where's the background research, the subtle interplay, the soul-searching, the agonising, the gradual building of the character, and final integration of it into the director's overarching concept? Look; I'm not knocking all of that. It's very desirable and once in a blue moon it happens. But I've seen performances in weekly rep (not whole plays but individual actors' performances), which I haven't seen bettered in the West End or anywhere. And it doesn't have to ruin you. Well of course I've got to believe that, but just to prove it I saw Mona Washbourne in a West End play and remarked to a friend what a marvellous truthful and yet inventive performance she was giving. I was told she'd been a Court Player for years. I was so encouraged that I wrote and told her what a joy it was for someone stuck in a weekly rep to know that it could lead to her sort of work. And it does teach you some things: attack, how to feel the shape of a play and know when it's your turn to carry it, confidence, versatility. You get to play an enormous variety of parts, and if you do them as honestly as you can they're bound to teach you something.

Nevertheless I made constant attempts to get out. From time to time I'd put myself out of work and go up to London to trail round the agents, cycling to save fares. With my smart hat and my high heels in the basket, I'd pedal round the West End, wobbling among the buses. Then it was up and down bare wooden staircases (all agents' offices are on the top floor) to ask if there was anything they could suggest me for or – wild hope – if they'd like to be my personal manager. On one of those forays I came across a door marked "Old Vic Management Office". I peered inside; just the usual bare wood stairs. I parked my bike, donned my hat and shoes and climbed up. Three doors on the first landing, and from one of them the sound of voices. No reply to my timid knock, so I pushed the door open and peered in. Three men were standing on the far side of a large empty room. John Burrell, Tyrone Guthrie and Laurence Olivier. They stopped talking and turned. A pause, then "Yes?" said Tyrone Guthrie. "Er," I said. "Er…" "Yes, dear?" "Well, – any work?" The next pause seemed even longer. Then, "I should write in, dear," said Guthrie kindly. "Yes," I said. "Yes. Thanks very much. Yes." I had to wheel my bike for quite a way before my knees stopped knocking.

Back to Harry Hanson, then. And £12 a week, my show of independence having paid off. Money's funny in this profession. You can get two thousand a day for a film (well that's the most I've ever got) and next week be on shares in a show over a pub and lucky to take home ten quid. Years after I finally left Harry H, I was playing Judith in "Hayfever" on shares in a freezing little theatre in Farnham, and I met Harry's manager on a train. "How much would you want to come back?" "£25." "Oh dear, is that your lowest?" "Not exactly. Three and ninepence this week."

That was in the icy winter of 1947 and not only was the theatre freezing but the railway lines, so that the journey after the show took four hours and, having nothing to read, I started to write a play. Before we get into that though, there's ENSA – The Entertainments National Service Association. My first job with them was as Maria in "Twelfth Night", a rather dire production we inflicted on the troops in England and Wales. I had a lovely time though, enjoying the part and getting on famously with the 80% homosexual company. I'd taken up riding, the ideal way to see the countryside, and when I saw the Menai Straits, bright blue sky and sea and the castle with its moat full of daffodils, I found tears in my eyes. So perhaps I was a sensitive soul after all and not the coarse-grained clown my director seemed to find me. She'd worked with Robert Atkins, which you'd have thought would have accustomed her to robust acting, but she obviously found me far too common. "But Maria's a maid," I protested," a servant." "She's a *lady's* maid, that's a very different thing." "But I'll never get the laughs if I don't go for the earthiness of it." "The laughs are not important." (Grandma thou should'st be living at this hour.) "In fact you're getting far too many laughs." So she stood in the wings and glared, shaking her head in fury every time there was a chuckle, until mercifully it was time for her to leave. I daresay I was over the top but I was trying to cheer things up. It's one of my failings to think I've got to rescue a play if it seems to be dragging. John Bennett once complained, "Marge, you weren't only playing your part and everyone else's, you were playing the scenery!" But the show really wasn't the stuff to give the troops. One of them confided in me that they'd been warned that anyone who left the hall would be put on a charge, and once they actually locked them in. It made you feel guilty really. All these poor chaps far from home, stuck in barracks and subjected to this.

The other two women were much more to the director's taste, Viola desperately earnest and Olivia very ethereal, not to say prissy. I got on quite well with them but found my real mates among the gay chaps who were great fun in the digs, really letting their hair down and accepting me into their fraternity. I had to remember all the girls' names they went by. My great friend in the company though, and for many years afterwards, was one of the two straight men, Leonard Trollope, vaguely related to the author. What a lovely man! Enthusiastic, learned, mischievously caustic, unpretentious and above all droll! "What is the first thing you look for in a man, Margery?" asked Viola. "To make me laugh." "Not **all** the time surely!" She was really shocked. Leonard professed to have a crush on me but as he was outstandingly happily married neither of us took it seriously and we had a great time together. He was madder on Shakespeare than anyone I've ever known, had read the whole lot and not just once. He'd go straight through the collected works and start again, finding new riches each time, he assured me, even in "Pericles" and "Titus Andronicus" and so on. He loved acting too but happily acknowledged that he wasn't all that good at it. When I went to stay with him and his wife I found a framed letter in the lavatory. It was from Martin Harvey, saying "Dear Mr Trollope, Thank you for rehearsing with us but regretfully we have decided that Guildenstern should not be quite such a tall man."

Chapter 5

I had hoped one ENSA job would lead to another but it didn't so I was in the doldrums again, this time demonstrating a con trick of a silver cleaner in the Ideal Home Exhibition and other trade fairs. It was a small sheet of metal which you immersed in water and a dash of washing soda, then plunged the precious silverware in, and when you fished it out it was all shiny and beautiful. You could do the same thing with milk bottle tops but most people didn't know that, so they handed over the bracelets and rings and of course when they got them back they felt committed to buying the product. It was sad to see how easily people were conned but it didn't pay badly and it kept me in London, so I could afford to cheer myself up by going to the gods in the theatre now and then. Favourite was the Old Vic. Not just for the shows but I could afford the pit there. The Vic had been my haunt as a kid. Vera and I had discovered it when we were thirteen and saw everything they did, often more than once. It was ninepence early doors in the gallery and fivepence late, and my God were they vintage years! Gielgud, Ashcroft, Richardson, Evans, Martita Hunt, Olivier – all the greats and lots of the good – all in monthly repertory. I kept a critical diary of all the performances, which thank God I've lost. Dear Harcourt Williams had the modesty and kindness to send a detailed reply to a scathing crit I sent him of his production of "The Shrew". As I complained about the inclusion of the Christopher Fry prologue, I was faulting Shakespeare as well as him!

John Gielgud was naturally the one Vera and I were mostly in love with. It started with "Richard II" which we saw three times, but he was wonderful in the sort of parts he never played later. Hotspur, for instance, all fire and light and funny to boot, and Sergius in "Arms and the Man." We hung about the stagedoor, not daring to speak but trailing him until he got into a cab. Then we took to writing letters from him, as if we were someone he was having an affair with. When Clem found these I was had up before her and Dad for an explanation. I felt I'd rather be suspected of "carrying on" than laughed at, so I remained dumb. I wonder if they really thought I was heavily into sex at thirteen? It wasn't so common then so they probably dismissed it as me being my usual inexplicable self.

Vera and I had now graduated to the pit, or rather to a ledge which stuck out nearer the stage. We were such regulars there that Lilian Baylis, passing through in her academic cap and gown to the royal box where she was rumoured to eat, if not actually cook, her dinner, would sometimes give us her twisted smile and a word.

Lord, we were lucky! What a way to see Shakespeare for the first time, and in such fresh, ungimmicky productions. Shakespeare's birthday was the greatest of larks. Not only all the stars coming back with their party pieces but a wonderful romp at the end. Once it was a pantomime, with Tyrone Guthrie a six-foot knobbly-kneed fairy and Lillian herself answering a dramatic cry of "Ha! I conceive ....!" With a snappy "You can't do that there 'ere!" It wasn't only Vera and I who were so innocent then; it was the whole world.

Thirty-five years later I met our idol. We were both working in the same TV studios in different plays, and as my director and fellow-actor were friends of his we all had dinner together in the canteen. He protested that he couldn't stay more than five minutes, he was too exhausted, and then proceeded to keep us enthralled and amused for a good hour and a half. When I could get a word in, I said, "I was in love with you when I was thirteen."

"Oh my dear," said that clipped but mellifluous voice, "What a mistake!"

Then ENSA came through after all with a wonderful job – a chance to go to the Middle East. This would be only the third time I'd been abroad. First with Vera, when we were twenty and saved up for a fortnight in Normandy, then, a few months before the War, Grace and I went to Vienna to stay with some Jewish people we were hoping to get over to England. Bert, who was now a cameraman, had met a Jewish girl in Austria while he was filming "The Constant Nymph" and after the Anschluss she wrote begging him to find a way of getting her and her sister out. There was a method of getting around immigration authorities which was quite widely used at the time. First you put advertisements in the papers offering domestic service jobs at low rates and with unattractive conditions. Then, when there were no British applicants, you got the Austrians to write saying they'd seen the advertisement and would be happy to fill the post. You took their letters and the advertisements to the authorities and got them permits. Looking back it seems unlikely the Foreign Office was convinced by all these shenanigans but perhaps the climate of opinion was sympathetic so one got away with it. Anyway we got them a couple of permits and then they wrote and asked us to come and stay with them for a week before they got out, so Grace and I set off on a rather rough boat and train journey. We missed our connection at Cologne because of the stupid German trick of making "halb acht" mean half past seven instead of half past eight, and found we had six hours' wait in the middle of the night. We didn't fancy waiting in a deserted station so we asked a policeman (Grace knew a bit of German) if there was a cheap lodging house. He seems to have directed us to a knocking shop, as there were loud comings and goings all through the night. Anyway, there was a lock on the door so we got a bit of intermittent sleep and caught our train. We needed direction at an interchange station so Grace primed me with the right enquiry and sent me off to get help from what we took to be a railway official. He turned out to be a Nazi officer and no help at all. In Vienna our hostesses did their very best to show us the town and give us a good time, taking us to the gates of parks and museums and waiting outside, not even allowed to sit on the 'Juden Verboten' labelled public benches. We knew all about that of course, but it was gut-wrenching when you actually saw it. When it came time to leave, the girls asked if we'd conceal some gold in our luggage so that they would have some means of support when they got to England. This was mainly in the form of bracelets which we wore under our long-sleeved tightly buttoned blouses, and coins buried in our powder boxes. Going through two sets of customs was a bit sweaty but we had no trouble and in fact the only really alarming moment came when, waking from sleep in the train at 5 a.m., I found a fellow passenger's hand up my skirt. He sprang back into his seat and brightly pointed out the castles on the Rhine so I pretended I hadn't noticed but didn't get to sleep again. The Austrian girls came over all right, claimed their gold and eventually got to Canada.

Chapter 6

Going abroad with ENSA meant you had to be enrolled as a honorary lieutenant and were issued with a uniform, subtly different from a real one, but it didn't stop soldiers saluting you in the street and making you feel a fraud. The play seemed a strange choice for the troops, "Nine Till Six", set in a dress shop with an all-female cast. Perhaps they thought, "Never mind the play, get some glamorous girls out there," and it certainly worked at that level. Some of the girls were real beauties and as they were playing mannequins there was a certain amount of discreet undressing. I was playing a poor girl who borrowed a dress for a night out, and at every single performance, as I stealthily snatched the dress from the rail, some wit in the audience would shout "Clifty waller!" And every single night in the mess after the show someone would buttonhole me with "Wasn't it a hoot when that chap shouted clifty wallah! That's Arabic for thief you know." "Oh really? How funny. No wonder they laughed." The mess parties got to be a bit of a chore after a while. I took to buttonholing the padre and arguing about religion. Well it made a change from "How long have you been out?" and "What did you do in civvy street?" Some of the girls were much better at it. They sang Noel Coward songs and told funny stories and generally did what we were supposed to be out there to do.

It was some time until we got the play out to Egypt though. We hung about so long in London waiting for transport that the War caught us on the hop and came to an end. Of course we joined the general rejoicing but we were a bit worried. Won't we go after all? But it was okay, there were plenty of servicemen still out there, and perhaps even more in need of distraction, so we were eventually given our jabs and put on the Winchester Castle, having been told that we were our country's ambassadors, should beware of mixing with the natives, and anyone who got pregnant would find herself on the next ship back.

We landed at Port Said and at once everything was wonderfully foreign, fascinating and exciting. We hadn't yet picked up our minder so, as we went down beside the Suez Canal, it was possible to sit on the steps of the train, dangling your legs and exchanging shouts and waves with the children who lined the route, throwing them tidbits and once – "My God, what's that they're selling? It is! It's bananas!" Hadn't seen one in England for a good five years. Then there were mirages and date palms and men ploughing with oxen and camels. All straight out of the Bible.

In Cairo our minder was waiting for us; Jock, a burly Scottish sergeant. After settling us in startlingly luxurious quarters, he took us on a trip round the city, initiating us into the proper way to deal with beggars, or indeed any importunate Arab. He'd been out there many years but his Arabic was restricted to "Imshi" and "Yalleroo" both of which meant "Get Out!"

Our luxury flats came with male servants, summoned with a clap of the hands or a cry of "Mohammed!" which seemed well over the top. You could sunbathe on the flat roof if you didn't mind all these young men peering over the parapet and giggling. It was a bit difficult to reconcile this sort of life with the Spartan quarters of the men we were supposed to be out there to serve, and the Egyptian people living and sleeping in the streets, but we soon got used to it. Almost at once our middle-aged leading lady got so ill she had to be sent home, and while we waited for her replacement we hung about very happily, swimming at the Gezeira Club, with its bright green golf course and cricket pitch surrounded by parched brown fields; off to Giza for the Pyramids and the Sphinx (it would smile for you if you paid for a cunningly sited flare), playing tennis, riding camels (on leading strings but that didn't stop me putting "Horse and camel riding" in my Spotlight ad), up the Nile in a felucca, touring the town in a horse-drawn gharri and whooping it up at night with troops of all nations. It was fortunate we weren't required to put on a show for some weeks as we went down one after another with the inevitable Gyppy tummy. I even became delirious and had to go to hospital, where the ants cleared out my two-pound box of chocolates in one night.

Finally we got our play on at the garrison theatre, and it was quite a success, particularly in the messes after the show. Our hosts were alternately officers and NCOs. We never went to the NAAFI to consort with the other ranks. In fact you were hard put to it to meet an ordinary soldier. The variety artists did better; you'd often see variety girls out on the town with privates or the like, though of course they couldn't take them to the Gezeira. I think I only ever went out with one private. Where was it? Oh yes, in Baghdad. He was an actor I'd worked with and he sent a note to the hotel. We went to a seedy bar and drank gin and orange with flies in it.

Ensa, Egypt 1946

He didn't seem to notice and I didn't want to increase his misery by being snooty so I drank them down. He'd only just come out and was hating every minute of it and pining to talk about the theatre. I remember he was pathetically grateful that I'd dressed up in "civvies". He said he'd only just learned not to call his uniform his costume. I met him later in London running a small suburban theatre, but he didn't employ me.

Ensa, Egypt 1946

After a couple of months we began to think Cairo hadn't much more to offer. We'd had a bit of excitement with a flood, which meant you had to be carried across roads by men who took the opportunity for a quick grope up your knickers, but on the whole the town was sultry, enervating and smelt of cooking oil, so we were wonderfully exhilarated by our next stop, Alexandria, with its rough seas, fresh air and intriguing mixture of races and nationalities.

The Summer Palace, where we were installed, was the haunt of King Faruk. Every night there he'd be at the side of the dance floor, sending his minions to invite the more glamorous girls to join him. Sometimes they went for a trip on his yacht and came back flashing a diamond or so, but there was always the risk they'd get shipped off back to England, even without getting pregnant. None of *our* girls engaged in these unsuitable activities – though I did fall violently and briefly in love with a young Jewish stockbroker – a strange aberration since he didn't even make me laugh. It was a curious life we lived, fêted and courted alike by British servicemen and the local bigwigs. I somehow got mixed up with a group of rich Greeks who were hoping to establish a multilingual theatre after the war and made me promise to come back and help them run it. Of course that came to nothing. Rich Arabs vied for our attention too. Once a fleet of cars took us into the desert for a picnic; champagne, whisky and a whole sheep stuffed with rice and nuts but not, thank God, the dreaded eye, which was supposed to be given to the guest of honour.

So we were spoiled rotten, though the work got tougher when we started doing one-night stands at remote posts, sometimes by the light of the car headlamps. The routine on these excursions was to set out early in the morning in our bus and make detours to take in some of the isolated outposts manned by two or three men. Sometimes these men had chosen that sort of posting, sometimes not. In either case the authorities felt they were in danger of becoming hermits, unsuitable for a return to normal life, and our job was to break this down and generally jolly them along. We tried but it didn't work. They obviously couldn't wait to see the back of us and had often turned away while we were still waving goodbye. Then we'd have to console our hurt pride with the Cyprus brandy as we were trundled and jerked along to the next abortive encounter.

We went to nine countries in all, though I can't remember in what order. Palestine, as it then was, was interesting because we were disliked and resented by the more political inhabitants, Jews and Arabs alike. The King David Hotel was blown up while we were in Jerusalem, which I suppose was the nearest we ever came to danger in the line of duty. I was rather less shocked by this explosion than by the performance of "Twelfth Night" I saw at the famous Habima Theatre. Perhaps Shakespeare doesn't translate well into Hebrew but they did seem to say "Shalom" an awful lot and really the show was even worse than our English one. Viola was well into her fifties and the comedy scenes were the broadest of unfunny slapstick. I've since thought that perhaps it was in an avant-garde style that I didn't appreciate but at the time I just wanted to get out. When I found the doors locked it seemed like retrospective revenge from our audience in England.

The country was very beautiful; orange groves and rocky hills smothered in anemones and asphodels. We duly made the pilgrimages to Nazareth and Bethlehem but somehow they were unimpressive. No-one seemed to have bothered to present them. Lord knows what they're like now. The Dead Sea came up to scratch though; you really could sit up in it and read the paper. And there actually were pillars of salt.

Beirut was the most beautiful city then, houses washed in pastel colours, ropes of oranges on the stalls and snow-covered mountains turning pink in the sunset. I suppose at least they can't have spoiled that. Syria was magic altogether – Damascus and the wonderful ancient Baalbek. You could actually swim in the rather murky sea too, and I had a Christmas Day dip, which always feels triumphant to us English. I remember thinking on the ride back from Baalbek "My God, I'm lucky! I'm so brimful of happiness if anyone tilted me I'd spill!" I was engaged at the time to a captain in the Remount Depot whom I'd met hunting jackals in Palestine, crashing about and ruining their orange groves. I feel guilty now about hunting but we didn't actually kill anything. What the army was doing with all those horses I can't imagine. They'd sent over to England for a dozen or so hounds too. Nice use of the taxpayers' money.

"Nine to Six" had finished by now and I was doing a four-hander with a very good comedy part, so I wasn't too devastated when my "fiancé" wrote to say he was terribly sorry and he hoped I wouldn't mind too much, but he'd married someone else.

Eventually I decided it was time to go back to England and get on with my career. I did, and was out of work for nine months (theatrical work that is) so I had to keep my end up with some very odd jobs. A communist friend persuaded me to be an English tutor to a member of the Bulgarian Embassy or Legation or whatever. I protested that I had no teaching skills or indeed much knowledge of English syntax, but this didn't seem to matter. It was rather like Miss McGuire's or Our Lady of Lourdes, never mind the qualifications, just so long you're politically (or religiously) correct. "You speak the language, don't you?" he said, "You'll be fine." I wasn't.

I bought a few books and mugged up as much as I could, but those two-hour sessions, nose to nose with a portly, black-jowled, middle-aged Bulgarian who fixed me with a look alternately challenging and baffled, were among the most agonising in my life. I had hoped to get away with a little reading and conversation, but though his grasp of the language was minimal he was an ardent student of the grammar and I was continually called upon to parse and analyse or explain the difference between the subjunctive and the conditional. After a month of this agony he announced there was to be a test at which I was to examine him before a panel. "What will happen if you fail?" I asked in despair. He shook his head gravely. "There will be criticism." When the test came he seemed unmoved but I went to pieces. Confronted by two men and a large woman in a pinstripe suit, I waffled and havered and finally with a desperate "Well I think that's enough, don't you? He's really done very well." I fled. I can't imagine that he passed and I sometimes worry what form the criticism took.

An only slightly less painful way of earning a bob or two was to take over the acting class of fellow actors when they got a job. A day-release class of thirty-five bored teenagers who'd obviously opted for drama as the least demanding course, greeted my attempt at relaxation exercises, which I'd hoped would take up half an hour or so, with cries of "Oh no Miss! Not all that knees bend stuff!" As there were only four copies to be had of any one play I ended up telling exaggerated anecdotes of theatrical disasters and laying claim to knowing all the stars. I also taught at the Italia Conti School, which had produced Noel Coward and Gertie Lawrence. My pupils were mainly kids who were earning a fortune in TV commercials and felt quite rightly I had nothing to teach them.

Chapter 7

Then I went into panto. I'd signed up for some lessons in a tatty singing and dancing school and when the kids in the class were asked to join a company taking "The Babes In The Wood" on a three weeks' tour I was asked to go as second boy (Will Scarlet) and tutor-chaperone. I had one point number which didn't require too much of a voice so I reckoned I'd get away with it,

We were to open at Wells so we assembled at Marylebone, and when I'd finally got the kids settled in the train, I looked out of the window and saw this amazingly good-looking young man with a fiddle case. Can he possibly be our musical director, I wondered. He was, and I made sure we sat together on the train. He wasn't only good looking, he was friendly and enthusiastic, and by the time we got to Wells I was well and truly smitten. I suppose you could say I practically flung myself at him. And – miracle – he responded. By the end of the three weeks' tour we were what's now known as an item. Well, not quite. Instant, casual sex wasn't quite so automatic in those days. Or perhaps it was and I didn't know. Anyway there wasn't all that much time for dalliance. All the kids got lice in their hair and as the only remedy I knew was liquid paraffin we had a chorus of drowned rats for a while; then our principal boy, who was pregnant, fell down and was off for the two Saturday shows, so Will Scarlet vanished and I became Robin Hood, with all her songs. That was the night the local amateur operatic company asked us to their dance. "Great show," said my partner. "Pity about your cold." And I had to 'tutor' the kids in the mornings. Luckily none of them was bright enough to show me up, and no-one ever came to check us.

With all this going on and two shows a day, it's a wonder Peter and I (that was his name, Peter Daminoff) ever got together. I do remember a fairly torrid session in a freezing shelter on Seaford seafront but mainly we talked like mad and found we agreed about everything, music, acting, politics, the state of the world, the state of the show. He was over in England from Toronto, and sharing a flat in London with fellow Canadians. I think, though I didn't know this at the time, they were all on their way to the Soviet Union or Eastern Europe. Their forebears had escaped from Russia or thereabouts in Czarist times and the descendants wanted to send their children back, now that the wonderful communist state had arrived. So they were all, including Peter, really just in transit. They were all pretty young too. Peter was 21 (though he said 25). I was 35 (and said so). I'd got to that age without ever thinking of getting married or ever much wanting to. I'd seen all the marriages, family ones and others, and thought yes, very nice but not for me. But when Peter asked me I didn't hesitate for a moment, I just said yes. I think he was a bit startled. "Just like that?" he said. Perhaps he'd just been trying out the idea and didn't expect to be snapped up quite so quickly. But I wanted him. I wanted to grab him and hang on to him. I suppose you could call it being madly in love.

We got married twice. Once at the registry office in Hampstead, and once in the Russian Orthodox church in Victoria. That was cheating, because neither of us had a religion, but Peter was desperate to be married in Russian, so I went along with it, even going for instruction from a Orthodox priest, who told me marriage wasn't just about romance but also about darning socks and keeping a clean kitchen. We had the full works, with men chanting, and us parading round the church with crowns held over our heads. Kate and Grace came with their kids, one of whom livened things up with audible comments and wolf-whistles. We lived for a while in my tiny attic flat, then I borrowed

£200 from Dad, engaging to pay him back £6 a week, and we moved to Chelsea in a road leading down to Albert Bridge.

Peter was really very talented, playing fiery gipsy music and hot fiddle as well as classical stuff, and got various jobs, one in a Mayfair restaurant, wandering round the tables playing schmaltzy stuff and graciously accepting tips. (A waiter told him if anyone had the sauce to offer coins he should "accidentally" drop them on the floor.) Prostitution, but it paid Dad's six pounds a week rent. He didn't have a dinner jacket, so we bought a blue satin shirt and I made him a purple cummerbund. Come to think of it I made two more so he must have got up a trio for a gig here and there. I couldn't seem to get any proper work so I went waitressing in Forte's open-air café, just over the bridge. I got sacked as usual, but this time for stealing. It turned out the chap who sacked me was on the fiddle and I was the fall guy.

Somewhere about this time I'd finished the play I'd started on the train back from Farnham. It was an amiable little piece about life in digs and, as one of the characters had lesbian leanings, I was called to the censor's office. They were very sweet, thought it a delightful play, but couldn't I give the woman a mother fixation instead? I said I probably could, but in the event I didn't need to because I sent the play to Oldham, which was a club theatre at that time and didn't have to bother with the censor. They did it proud and we went up for the first night. Sitting in an audience and hearing your lines get the laughs you'd hoped for takes a lot of beating.

Then Peter went to Toronto for a brief visit to his parents and I didn't hear from him for five months. I wrote and got no answer. Wrote again: nothing. I even sent a telegram "Shostakovich" which was our joke version of "Shto s boyu", Russian for "What's going on?" When it failed I decided he'd left and I wasn't going to chase him. I was broke by now and too low to make much effort at anything so I took a job at Selfridges for £6 a week plus 1% commission. Horrible, horrible! Hard-faced supervisors on your tail all the time in the hope of cutting down on pilfering, which was rife. At first I was always producing alien pieces of merchandise from under the counter, "What's this camera doing here?" (We were a toy department.) "Put it back! It's mine, nothing to do with the shop. Put it back!" I was two hours late back from Christmas and they docked my entire holiday money. I should have done a bit of pilfering to get my own back. Still I stayed on, somehow unable to summon up the strength to extricate myself. Then one night I heard a noise on the landing and there was Peter. Looking a bit fat. Did he explain what he'd been up to? Not really. Did I ask? Hardly at all. I probably knew, without letting myself face it, that this was a marriage that wouldn't bear too much investigation. Enjoy it while it lasts and don't look too far ahead. So we went on as before, getting jobs which separated us from time to time but enjoying life when we were together. I joined Amersham rep, which was commutable from London, except on Saturday night, when the cast conspired to cut whole chunks out of the play so we could catch the last train home.

Then I heard that Walthamstow was looking for a week's panto and, having a few weeks off and a musician husband, I asked for and got the booking. I'd got a script I'd written earlier for an amateur company – "Babes in the Wood" again – so I rustled up a few singing actors, kids for a chorus, and variety acts for the obligatory grande finale. Peter gathered a small scratch orchestra, the Amersham scenic artist came to my rescue with a few leafy flats and a backcloth and we rehearsed for a fortnight and threw it on. It was pretty dire, and got more or less the reception it deserved. Peter's gipsy fiddle act was greeted with a hail of boiled sweets, and when our Sheriff of Nottingham was too drunk to perform, I stripped off his costume, forced it on to an actor friend who'd happened to drop in and shoved the poor chap onstage to wing and busk the part. Still, we came away with £270, and all in notes. We took them to bed with us. So now I was in management, and when I heard that Bangor, County Down, was looking for a company to do a ten weeks' summer rep season, I applied and got accepted, going back to work at Amersham in the meantime.

Now at this time neither Peter nor I was actually in the Communist Party, but he got the chance of going on a C.P. organised trip to play in Bulgaria for a week or so. I thought maybe he'd disappear again, but no, he came back all right, only he said he'd met a girl over there and he wanted a divorce. This was a real surprise. He'd never shown any interest in any other women, even those who made a play for him, and our love life hadn't seemed in trouble. But no, he was adamant; he'd met this girl and he wanted a divorce. Oh, and would I arrange it? It was my country after all and I'd know how these things were managed.

Oddly enough I did, and perhaps this is as good a moment as any to take a break from all this angst and explain how I knew. It was all Grace's doing. Years before, when I was quite young, she was living in the country among a rather posh set of people, one of whom was trying to get his wife to divorce him so he could marry his mistress, but she – the mistress – wasn't keen on being seen as a co-respondent. So Grace proffered my services. For £20 I could spend a night in a hotel with him, and provide the evidence. Well it seemed harmless enough, and £20 was a lot of money, so off we went to Maidenhead, where Grace introduced us, with many a nervous chuckle and quip, then promptly moseyed off, leaving us to check into the hotel and eat a very stilted dinner. (He was amazingly dull, how could two women quarrel over him?) Then we repaired to our room, he to the armchair, me to the bed. Next morning he woke me to say he'd ordered room service and could I roll about on the bed and rumple it up a bit. The maid brought the breakfast and we asked her some silly questions in the hope she'd remember us, I got my twenty quid and we parted. I thought that was that, but then I was summoned to appear in court. "Did you spend the night with Mr So-and-So?" "Yes." "And did you have sexual intercourse with him?" "Oh yes." So now I was a perjurer. You'd have thought it would have been worth another twenty quid, but no.

Anyway, back to my tragi-comic, ill-considered marriage. I did indeed arrange the divorce and he was free to go, whether to Bulgaria or elsewhere I didn't know. About twenty years later I got a letter from him c/o Equity, saying he'd seen me on telly and was over here with the Toronto Symphony Orchestra. I was half tempted to go and spy at the concert, just to see if he'd run to fat. I did rather hope so.

I had five weeks to plan and cast the Bangor season, and as I was still working at Amersham to build up a bit of capital it was tough going. Therapeutic, though – took my mind off my personal woes. Then the final blow: he'd cleaned out our joint account before he left. So I set off on the boat with my company with just £250 in the bank. We travelled steerage, night crossing, no berths, but angelically they didn't complain. After the first week, with rehearsal salaries and rent for the theatre, I was cleaned out, so we needed a bumper opening week. Of course we didn't get it, but here's where the magic of Ireland kicked in. I'd transferred to the Bangor branch of my London bank, so I went to them. "I need a loan," I said. "Ah yes, Miss Mason isn't it? London said you'd be coming. A loan, you say?" "Yes, only I've no collateral, nothing to – " "Sure we'll not be needing any of that. Didn't London say we were to look after you? How much would you be needing?" No wonder I love Ireland.

Business looked up after a while and by penny pinching and paying scandalously low salaries I managed to get through the ten weeks without getting into debt. I put on the play Oldham had done, trusting the long arm of the censor didn't stretch to Ulster, and another one I'd hastily finished, happy, like Clem in the past, to save on royalties. I was disconcerted to find during rehearsals of the second play that the first act only ran twelve minutes but I hoped it might stretch with laughs and it did, to a respectable twenty-three. The play went over very well, in fact it did next to top business for the whole season. (It might have been the bank holiday week.) Manning the box office at lunch-hour, I had a moment of disbelief. "Good Lord," I thought. "All these people queuing up (well, eight of them). They wouldn't be there but for me." It's a strange feeling: a mixture of power and a dread of being found out.

Chapter 8

Then I kidded the Mayor of Bangor to turn one of his auction rooms into a properly equipped theatre, and to let me try to establish a permanent rep in the town, and a year later I brought a company over and opened the New Theatre. I ran it for fifteen months and it was the most challenging, exhausting, rewarding, frustrating, heart-breaking, heart-warming time of my life. I couldn't have done it anywhere else; the Bangor people are amazing. It's a little seaside town, partly a dormitory for Belfast, far too small to support a rep out of season and a bit dodgy even in the summer months. Since it's so far North – next stop Greenland – it's light until nearly eleven and to my fury people would still be on the beach when they should have been in my theatre. Still there was a hard core of real theatre-lovers who rallied round. A wonderful man, a Mr Collings, started a car stickers campaign. "Have you been? I go every week." Alas, I never met him, though he was reported as claiming we'd been to bed together, because we'd been laid out next to each other as blood donors. Then other enthusiasts formed a supporters' club and not only manned my coffee bar and did my ushering but organised all sorts of fundraising activities. Still, I teetered on the verge of collapse, financially and physically. I've never been good at delegating and anyway I was paying such peanuts that I couldn't ask anyone to do anything extra, so I directed all the plays, played many of the leads, did the publicity, chased round for programme advertisements, manned the box office in the lunch hour, once finished the set when my scenic artist was drunk, chose the plays and did the paperwork and finally – but this was a secret – wrote the reviews for the two local papers. We'd changed our opening night from Monday to Thursday, hoping to catch holidaymakers twice in one week, and a delegate from the firm which printed both papers appeared. My opening was now after their press date, he said, and he was wondering, could I perhaps write the reviews myself? It seemed not only unethical but a faggot above a load, but of course I agreed. My experience with the Impartial all those years ago stood me in some sort of stead, but inevitably I'd drive it up to the last minute and be in the throes of dress rehearsal on the Thursday afternoon when a figure would sidle up with a muttered plea for the copy. We kept it hidden even from the company so if one of them was being difficult I had a secret weapon. I only very rarely used it and of course the review always finished on an upbeat note with a firm recommendation to go along and see a rattling good show.

As the weather got nasty and the town went into hibernation I cast round for yet more help and went to see the entertainment manager. "I expect you can guess what I want," I said. "Whatever it is you can have it," he answered without missing a beat. Irish magic again. It was small beer – unbelievably small against today's figures – but it saved my bacon. He gave me twenty pounds a week, the Arts Council matched it, and I struggled on.

The shows varied. Some were a bit dodgy but on the whole we kept a fair standard. Difficulties were compounded by there being hardly any actors in Northern Ireland outside those employed in two small Belfast companies. So if I wanted to do an Agatha Christie – not that I did but she brings 'em in – with a dozen or more in the cast, I had to bring people over from England which I couldn't afford or – last recourse and don't let Equity catch me – engage an amateur.

There were some good ones about – Colin Blakely was a marvellous Will Mossop in "Hobson's Choice" for the Bangor Drama Society before he went on to be a star in London and the world – but I didn't seem to get them, or more likely they couldn't function on a week's rehearsal. So that restricted the choice of plays. As did the public taste. Of course some aficionados would support us come what may, but looking at my records I see that "The Glass Menagerie" hit rock bottom and "Honeymoon Beds" came second only to the panto.

All this was taking place in 1953-5 when, though the sectarian divide was there, it was still possible for an innocent from over the water to be only mildly aware of it. I was shocked to see the police with guns, though not, I was assured, for ordinary criminals, just for terrorists. They didn't seem to think this was as funny as I did, and when one of my actors was hauled off the street for questioning because he was wearing running shoes, I began to realise I had a lot to learn about Northern Ireland. Then there was the dubious reception given my new coffee bar, with its smart green and white décor. I was told that wasn't the wisest colour scheme, so I added orange curtains and it seemed to do the trick. It was felt worthy of comment that my box office clerk and my cleaner were both Catholic – "and she's got these two children by an American, did you know?" So that when the local ASM I'd hired turned out to be C of I, I thought that would even things up. Until a local reporter came round asking me if she was good living, when I flew into a rage. "What the hell do I know about her private life? What's it got to do with me or you?" He was taken aback. "No," he said, "I just meant – well she seems the type." Apparently, Good Living is a sort of label given to people of a pious and circumspect character. There's another Northern Irishism I like: "He's not wise," they say, meaning he's completely bonkers. I decided my best course was to leak the news discreetly that I was an atheist, which caused hardly a ripple. At least I wasn't a Papist or a Prod. They're such lovely people, the Northern Irish, just not wise.

After I'd been going some time, the Arts Council, or CEMA as it was called at that time, engaged me to take a production of Priestley's "Eden End" on a fortnight's tour of one-night stands, so

I set up a play to leave behind in the theatre, with a two-hander to follow, to be directed and starred in by Jimmy Ellis, who'd been a pillar of the company so far. Halfway through his rehearsals he and his co-star announced they couldn't open on time, they wouldn't be ready, but I turned on them with such scorn and fury that they thought better of it. Then the rest of the company and I set off with a car and a van, some new scenery and a pukka new leading character actor. Once we were out on the road, he got drunk quite a lot of the time and could only be coerced into turning up for the show by the withholding of his salary and luggage and the threat of legal action. Which naturally didn't endear me to him or help our performances as estranged husband and wife rediscovering their love. All the same I enjoyed the tour. I hadn't set foot outside Bangor for a year and although many Ulster small towns are hardly distinguishable from each other it was great to see something of the countryside, and meet new and welcoming people, and bliss not to have a single line to learn for two whole weeks.

Things were still rocky though and the owner of the theatre, the man I'd persuaded to set it up in the first place, began to feel restive. Unknown to me, four members of my company approached him and persuaded him they could do better, so he sought to terminate my lease. There was a certain amount of outrage in the town but I knew in my heart by this time that a year-round rep wasn't a viable proposition in a town of that size, so I bowed out. Not before the panto though. This was the one fortnight in the year when we were sure of full houses so I decided to recoup what I could, pay all my debts and go out with a bang. Alone in the theatre after the last night I got steadily drunker as I packed everything up and took a last look round. Finally I stood on the stage, shouted defiance and hurled anything I could lay my hands on into the auditorium. Next day I tried to seem cheerful as kind friends were taking me to the boat but I had the father and mother of a hangover.

Chapter 9

I had a rather thin time after this. I was pretty well run to rags and had no idea where to go next. More weekly rep? Oh God save me! And anyway half the reps had died with the advent of telly. All right, see what's doing in telly. So off round the agents again. Nothing on offer except crowd work. Why not? It pays and it's acting. It's not and it's humiliating. It shouldn't be. With the endemic and obliviously incurable unemployment among actors, wouldn't it be better if instead of handing out leaflets at street corners, clearing café tables or demonstrating gimmicky rubbish at trade fairs, we could earn our keep between jobs by exercising our craft in the background without sacrificing status or self respect? I thought I could but I was wrong. We were bodies and nothing else. After two pretty devastating experiences, one when a member of the cast turned out to be one of my Bangor actors whom I'd advised to give up acting, and one when I was given two pounds extra and called "a proper pro" for having shaving soap squirted into my face, I decided this wasn't a good career move.

Help came from a fellow commie. Howard Goorney, who was going to be in the new Shelagh Delaney play at the Royal Court, got me an audition with Clive Barker, who'd been Joan Littlewood's sidekick at Theatre Workshop. This was the first time I encountered the new-style improvisation type of work. "There's a terrified stray cat marooned in the dress circle. Coax it down," said Clive from the stalls. Deciding that I was really auditioning for the type of work more than the part, I asked earnestly if it was a Persian or a tabby as I needed to visualize it. Then it was "Here, pussy, come along, pussy. No, don't jump! You'll hurt yourself. There, there – what a lovely purr!" and so on, and I got the part. The play wasn't quite finished when we started rehearsals. Shelagh, who'd had great success with her first play, "A Taste of Honey," was being cajoled and jockeyed into producing her second, so while we waited for the script we worked at the impro. In the play I was part of a double act, working-class Lancashire housewives. In the impro, we became lesbian policewomen, vying with each other to make an arrest. It was quite possible to pass rehearsal time amusingly like this even if it seemed to have little to do with the ultimate product, and perhaps I was learning new skills – who knew? Anyway when we finally came into London after four weeks on tour, during which we rehearsed every day, instructed occasionally, in the absence of any obvious aim, to "just kick it around and have fun", I found myself on a West End stage at last – well, very nearly.

Then in our last week John Dexter, who wasn't quite as grand as he later became, turned up in the dressing room and asked if I'd like to go to Worthing for a week to play Beaty's mother in "Roots". He'd directed the Wesker trilogy containing this play at the Court and, as a favour to Mary Miller, who'd later played Beaty in an excerpt with the author, had agreed to direct her in it if she could find a suitable rep. This was the first time I'd worked with a really good director and although it wasn't entirely pleasant – I don't think I'd be alone in finding Dexter a waspish man – it was certainly interesting and constructive. He slaughtered me when I was having a ball in my big scene. "What's all this middle-class hysterical shit? Just say the lines." And later, "Never mind the acting, just get the potatoes peeled." Very good advice. I've tried to keep it in mind.

Then, still at Worthing, we were actually given two weeks to rehearse "The Corn is Green" with Emlyn Williams's son in his father's part and Flora Robson as the schoolteacher. They were taking it, but not us, on a South African tour and I suppose we were being used to run them in for the final production. Lèse-majesté it may be but it's no good pretending I took to Dame Flora. I'd admired her work for years, but working in a weekly rep company, with a director practically prostrate with awe, didn't bring out the best in her. "He's giving notes, dear," she'd say as she strolled off to her dressing-room, and any pause in rehearsal was liable to be filled by tales of public acclaim or the adulation of her fans. And she knitted all the time. Not actually while she worked but certainly while you did, clicking away. As Miss Moffatt, that quintessentially down-to-earth intellectual, she brought out all the emotional stops, with tears streaming down her face at the final curtain. In one of her little homilies during rehearsal, she told us her infallible method of summoning up tears. "I think of the Thetis disaster." Using the thought of those poor chaps choking to death in their submarine seemed pretty crappy to me. If the part doesn't make you cry, forget it. It's harder in film or telly of course where there's no atmosphere or continuity, but the better actresses manage it. Juliet Stevenson's the queen of genuine tears, snot and all. I bet she doesn't think of something else. An unfortunate thing happened on the first night. I was playing Mrs Watty, a comic part created by the brilliant Kathleen Harrison and a gift to anyone like me, who likes her laughs. As I flounced off with my final line I got a great big exit round, leaving Dame Flora with just one poignant line to end the play. I didn't mean to do it and of course I killed the round the next night, but it was a nice feeling to know I could bugger up her curtain if I wanted to.

Somehow these little forays into more classy work had got me an agent and he duly got me my first telly, in a long running soap, "Emergency Ward Ten." All tv was live then and I chose my tv debut to have my first real flat-out dry. Of course I'd dried and fluffed many a time in the theatre but I'd known how to get myself out of it. This time I embarked on a speech and immediately realised that I didn't know how it ended. I finished the first bit then stood there, in close-up, with two million people watching, while a strange tremor ran right up one side of my body and down the other. Then I heard the boy who was playing my invalid son, and who was of the "when you stop it's my turn" school, carry blithely on. It didn't take make much sense but even the director didn't seem to have noticed so my tv career wasn't blighted at the start. And I suppose if I can be said to have done any good work that's been my medium. I like it best too, though not so much now it's all on film. It's true that when you had two or three weeks' rehearsal there was a lot of hanging about but at least you got a sense of the play as a whole and a chance to get to know your fellow actors. Now you only see them when you're in a scene together, and when you're elevated to your own caravan you're even more isolated. Your driver stands in the meal queue for you and you don't eat in the dining bus, so make-up's the only social scene. That's where you get all the gossip.

Nearly all actors say they love the theatre best. Though not Patrick Troughton, who complained about "all that shouting night after night." But most say nothing can replace the rapport with an audience. I certainly revelled in it all those years in the wilderness, but the more prestigious my theatre work has become the more it seems to me to be beset with rôle-playing, self-indulgence and the pursuance of ever more precious techniques and gimmicks. In the world of tv and film these excesses are kept in check by a tight schedule and a crew of seasoned technicians who know what they're doing and get on with it. It's very satisfying working that way.

I was still out of work a lot of the time and doing odd jobs to pay the rent when the CP came to the rescue again. Not with a job but with an enormous room in Swiss Cottage for 17/6 a week. Bill was a real communist and refused to make money from rents. He'd got a large maisonette on lease from the Church Commissioners and when he decided to move he kidded them I was his sister-in-law and got the lease made over to me. So here I've lived for the last forty-eight years, in a large flat with a lovely garden, and if ever I were tempted to regret joining the Communist Party, which I don't, I'd only have to look around and be grateful. Not that that's why I joined. I believed in communism and still do, in spite of all the horrors and corruption and breath-taking inefficiency. It's not as if anything else works. I joined the Party shortly after Peter left. We'd spent quite a few Sunday mornings at Speakers' Corner, where he was knocked out to hear such revolutionary views so openly expressed, and after he left I went back to the Corner at a May Day rally and stepped up to the rostrum and joined. Believe it or not there were seven active and sizeable branches in Hampstead then, and I was enrolled in the Belsize Branch. I suppose I thought it would be just a nice intellectual talking shop with like-minded people but I soon found myself selling the Daily Worker on the street and trudging up and down high-rises with pamphlets. It was good though. The meetings were stimulating and the Comrades were lively and congenial, not at all the humourless zealots of popular conception. The first Aldermaston march was a knock-out. So many people with such urgent concern for the world! I was baffled by the new logo though. "What's it mean? It'll never catch on." In the next demo I plumped down in Whitehall next to Bertrand Russell (name-dropper) and was hauled away by a couple of policeman. "Look out, this one's heavy." (I wasn't, he was just being rude – fascist beast.) "Chalking" was fun too. No spray paint in those days, so "Hands off Guatemala" was a four-handed job. Three pots of paint, three brushes and a lookout for the police. Then the paraphernalia stowed away and a triumphant trip to the pub. I found lots of good friends among the Comrades as well as one or two lovers. I've sometimes had a rather worrying thought though. Fervent Catholic to ardent Communist. Couldn't show a tendency to blind faith, could it?

One of my activities in the branch was with the Socialist Sunday School. Some of the CP mothers had the idea of enrolling their kids in the School to enter the annual drama festival. I imagine this was one of our perennial efforts to establish a Broad Front with the Labour Party. So I wrote a play for fourteen children about war orphans in the Pestalozzi Village and we rehearsed it in my enormous room, which was fine except for the night when the girl I'd let the adjacent room to produced a still-born baby without warning or benefit of doctor, and the place was alive with ambulance men and police, while I tried to keep the rehearsal going and deflect the attention of the Labour Party mum who'd come along to help out. Anyway, we won the festival that year and the next, and some of the kids later went on to become pros. This was the first time that I wrote and directed a play for a specific cast, and later I went on to do it quite a lot, for money. I can't think why, as it's the most wearing and traumatic exercise imaginable, and though I'm sometimes fairly proud of the end product, I can't pretend I enjoy the process, and I'm not sure the actors do.

It was on a march (I wonder against what?) that Harry Landis persuaded me to play Sarah Khan, the Jewish Communist mother in Arnold Wesker's "Chicken Soup With Barley" at Unity, the left-wing amateur theatre. The only thing most people know about Unity is that Paul Robeson acted there but in fact it's had a great history and a whole lot of adventurous and innovative work was done there while the commercial theatre was playing safe. Their "living newspapers" were often brilliant. I remember when the two crises of Suez and Hungary coincided, the place was full of Communists and Conservatives tearing up their Party Cards!

I wasn't sure if I could do Cockney Jewish but I wandered round the East End markets, and got the hang of it fairly well, and of course Sarah's a wonderful part. While I was doing it the BBC decided to do the Wesker Trilogy on television and I was offered the part I'd played at Worthing, the mother in "Roots". Then Charlie Jarrott, the director, whom I'd worked with before, couldn't find a Sarah to his liking so it was decided I should do it, which was great because Sarah's in two of the three plays. The only trouble was that I was playing it at Unity at night and rehearsing it for Charlie in the daytime, and when he came to the theatre he hated my performance and wanted me to do it differently. I trusted him so I did my best but it was a strange experience; one interpretation in the studio in the daytime and another in the theatre at night. Also I'd wricked my back carrying a rather large boy in the show and could hardly walk.

There was nearly a disaster during the tv rehearsals. At one point a crowd had to pass outside the windows of the Khan flat singing the Red Flag, and Harry Landis, who was also in the telly, and I were so distressed at the poor show they were putting up that we got the words duplicated and drilled them in it. The next morning Charlie met me in consternation. "What on earth have you done? They're demanding eighteen pounds extra for singing. They say they were handed the words and directed in it so it's not an ad lib." The BBC were furious and I could only placate them by trotting off to Equity and getting a ruling that did the extras out of their extra. Nice work for a Commie.

Arnold Wesker brought some of his family to one of our studio days and I entertained them in my dressing-room with my elderflower wine. His uncle from Hungary bowed over my hand and made a short speech in his native language which I took to be an appreciation of my performance. "Oh, tell him I'm thrilled," I was beginning, when Arnold interrupted with "Relax, he's just saying his name." The Trilogy was quite a big success on tv and I started playing so many Jewish parts that it looked as if I'd never play anything else. This was a nice time in my life. I'd just got my first car and I remember thinking, "Look at me! Driving to the BBC to rehearse a leading part! I suppose I'm what's called a successful actress."

I was quite successful for a while too, playing everybody's mother on tv. "A Family at War" made me the most hated woman in the country as I whinged away week after week. Patrick Troughton and I and Ian Thompson as our son were only supposed to be in the first three of 52 episodes but they decided to make the son missing instead of killed so I was able to continue to henpeck the long-suffering Patrick, carp at Lesley Nunnerley as my daughter-in-law, generally wallow in resentful self-pity and recriminations on and off throughout the series. For some reason this character attracted a lot of publicity and I was continually interviewed and photographed sitting on the bonnet of my white sports car, pulling a pint in Grace's pub, hanging from the bars in the gym, all as a contrast to the awful Mrs Porter. They even came and photographed me in my garden for a Radio Times series "Stars and Their Gardens". That was the first time I'd been called a star and I loved it. I was unashamedly chuffed to be recognised in the streets, even when hailed as "Old Misery Guts!" Patrick and I got on well too and there was talk of a comedy series for us, which of course came to nothing.

I even came to terms with Manchester, perhaps because I had digs with the lovely Marjorie Hoey, the pattern of what a landlady should be. She and Edna Newton of Billingham, who makes the creamiest orridge in the world, are my top landladies. I'm tempted to say my bottom one is the lady in Leeds who handed me the wrapping from the loaf as she led me to the outside loo. Marjorie's only blind spot was my driving; just because I knocked her wall down a couple of times. Patrick and I used to share driving up and down on weekends and he seemed confident enough with me, perhaps because he was a bit of a speed merchant himself, never able to resist doing the ton on a certain bit of motorway. We were pulled over by the police once in my car, not for any offences but because they were doing some sort of check. The dodgy thing was that among the luggage I'd flung onto the back seat was a large transparent plastic bag of marijuana. Pat had asked me to get some for him and although I'd long given up any hope of having it work for me I could still get hold of it easily enough – well everybody could. Pat had forgotten it was there so was quite happy to respond to the officers' excited recognition of him as an ex-Doctor Who. "Come on Pat, we're late already" I said, frantically looking round for something to throw over the bag. But they were still burbling on with "Who was the chap who took over from you? The one with all the hair?" Finally I put the car in gear and we were nearly on our way when, "Just a minute, just a minute." (Oh God!) "Did you say you came from London? Can I see your licence?" "What? Why?" "You're sure you're not from Luton?" "Luton?" "I live there. I'm sure I've seen you around." "I've never been to Luton in my life. I live in London. I'm an actress. I'm Mrs Porter, for God's sake!" "Who?" "Pat, tell him. We'll never get away. Tell him!" Pat did, but it so happened he didn't watch "A Family at War" so we left him only half-convinced I wasn't a secret denizen of Luton. He'd been a great "Dr. Who" fan though and thought Pat was the best of the lot, so one of us was happy, and Pat later said he'd had quite a good time with the pot.

Pot's never worked for me. I've sat stony-faced in too many parties while people giggled and chattered and dreamed around me so I've given up trying. LSD, now, that's a very different thing. I've had a hell of a lot of that, but not for fun, quite legitimately in a psychiatrist's clinic, mainlining every Tuesday for weeks on end. I'd developed migraine, which runs in the family, and was referred by my doctor to a clinic for, as I thought, hypnotism. The doctor said no, he was now using this new drug, lysergic acid diethylamide and he could treat me in his Chelsea clinic. It was quite a posh set-up, separate rooms and comfortable little beds. The nurse injected you and gave you some pills so you wouldn't go too mad, then left you for it to work. From time to time she or the doctor would come and see how you were getting on, I spent the whole six hours of my first visit crying uncontrollably and whimpering "They don't want me," with the doctor patting me occasionally and saying "Poor child." Next time I was born, twice. I'd shoved my head between the bed and the wall, and then I wrenched it out with a squawk and heard a voice say, "Pity it's a girl." Now this is nonsense. How would I understand words? But the doctor insisted. Everything I was experiencing now I had experienced before. It never happened any other way. I half believed him, though my faith was shaken some years later when a chap at a party told me he'd given birth to his sister under LSD. Still, the sessions at the clinic weren't all miserable and some of them were enlightening, or seemed so. Got shot of the fear of death for ever anyway. Unfortunately, the doc was a Freudian and kept insisting my trouble was that I wouldn't accept my femininity; I must face my penis envy. I tried. I found a dummy in the bed (a plant, or perhaps a left-over from a previous patient?) and dutifully put it between my legs and sprayed the room, but it didn't make me less resentful when I was rejected for a tv directors' course. ("A woman would have to be exceptional"; they actually said it.) Then he took to sitting with me rather longer and eventually tried a grope or so. I rather liked that – well of course I'd "transferred" to him by now – but when he sprang away as a nurse approached I lost faith, and as my migraine was no better I packed it in.

Then I found I missed it. Was I never to live at that transcendental level again? Kate's younger son, who's in the pop world, got me a couple of tablets but they were feeble stuff so I searched round and got another LSD doctor, a woman this time. She worked hard to convince me I was a lesbian. I said I'd nothing against the idea and indeed thought it might be an improvement on my love life so far, but I just didn't fancy it. She persisted for a further session, then she cut the cackle and got into bed with me, "Just for a cuddle." I got out in a hurry and she said the session was over, I could leave the money on the bedside table and she dared say I could find a cab. I was still heavily drugged and wandered about the West End in a daze before I finally got myself home. I should have reported her of course. I should have reported both of them, but the whole scene was so bizarre I let it slide. And perhaps it's something to have been fancied by weirdos of both sexes?

Things started to look up as bit then, and I was sent an exciting script written by Jack Rosenthal called, "Sadie, it's Cold Outside" which was hopefully to be the pilot of a new series. I saw the director about Sadie. and he said it was mine when they'd found me a suitable partner. Then I heard no more until I met Jack at the start of filming another of his scripts. "Sorry about Sadie," he said, and I found they'd cast it elsewhere. You never really get used to being treated like doo-doo but it's part of the game. Not that I blame Jack – authors get it too – it's "Them up There". However, the new script, "The Evacuees", was great – heartrending and funny – about a couple of Jewish boys, evacuated from the bomb-threatened city to be quartered on a well-meaning but uncomprehending woman. A good part – unsympathetic but with pathos, which Jack's good at. A good cast, too, with Maureen Lipman as the boys' mother. I hadn't worked with Maureen but I'd seen her long before in the little theatre Granada had next to their studios and I'd gone about then saying, "Who's that terrific girl playing the sister?" So when she got so famous I felt a bit of a talent scout. Also we had Alan Parker, no less, for a director and as we did it in Blackpool I could get in the rather chilly sea from time to time.

I don't know quite when I got elected to the Equity Council, but I do know I was absolutely useless. It was split down the middle between far-right and far-left, neither giving an inch or indeed listening to a word the other side said. And for some reason I was intimidated by them all. I sat there thinking "In a minute I'll say something," but the rows had been going on so long that everybody but me knew what they were about, so I was afraid of making a fool of myself. I did that in spades at the AGM, when I was put up to defend the Council on what seemed to me a fairly uncontroversial issue. It proved to have unsuspected political aspects and Tom Kempinski leapt up from the stalls and tore me to shreds. It didn't help that I agreed with everything he said and felt a traitor as well as a fool.

Maybe I'd been elected to the Council as the result of a fiery speech I'd made at the previous AGM on the subject of jobs for women. I remember it started, "I would like to open 'Fellow workers' like the last speaker, but I'm an actress, I don't work, so I'll say 'Mr Chairman and fellow members, first and second class.'" Then I got into my stride and really pitched into the Council for making no attempt to balance the ratio of jobs for men and women. There was a lot of loud agreement from the floor and a huge cheer at the end. The press, who were fed up with "Boycott South Africa" as the only newsworthy motion year after year, converged on me and the next day there were reports in The Times and The Standard. The Times heading "Actress topples Ancient Régime" caused confusion when a Comrade proudly showed it to a delegate from Bulgaria. She told him sternly that these topless fashions were considered decadent in her country. I told the Standard reporter to meet me at the Soho Labour Exchange, where I'd be among the many other actresses signing on. He did a full page piece headed "Down Among the Jobless Birds." Heigh-ho. Granada rang to ask for suggestions for plays packed full of women's parts, but of course there weren't any, that was the whole point, nothing but the inevitable "The House of Bernardo Alba." André van Gyseghem, who'd encouraged me to make the protest, said he wished I'd worn a pretty hat!

Feeling that raising my hand now and then wasn't contributing much to Council meetings I slithered out on some pretext or other. Politicians are a weird lot and actors playing them offstage seem to me to get a bit carried away with the part. In a meeting of three people in my flat I was addressed throughout as "Madam Chair".

Chapter 10

It was some time in the sixties that I did what some people consider the best thing I've ever done, "Talking to a Stranger". I'm not so sure myself. I'd like to think I've improved with time, and when they put it out again recently on BBC 4 I thought everyone was better than me, particularly Michael Bryant. But it was certainly one of the best things I've been in. Of course the quality started with the writing. John Hopkins, who'd been turning in consistently brilliant scripts for "Z Cars" among other things, broke new ground with four 90-minute plays looking at the same disastrous Sunday afternoon through the eyes of father, mother, son and daughter – Maurice Denham, me, Michael Bryant and Judi Dench. Some of the scenes in the parents' house were repeated in several episodes from different angles, and there were lots of excursions in time and place, one going back to the parents' crucial wedding night when my part was played by Ann Mitchell, who went on to do a lot of good work. I'm afraid I'm not giving anything like an idea of the complexity and brilliance of the script, or of its truthfulness and subtlety. It also had something you don't get nowadays, good long scenes. Page after page of dialogue, sometimes with just two people. Turn a page these days and they've cut to somewhere else. It also got masterful direction from Christopher Morahan, who'd obviously done intensive work on it. I remember him saying, "Put the cup down there because when we come to your story I'm shooting from the other angle." The plays went out on successive Sunday nights and caused a bit of a furore. There were rave reviews and several awards. I was put up for one but naturally it went to Judi – and rightly, she was marvellous in a much more complicated part than mine. I knew the mother as soon as I read the script and was able to feel pity as well as despair for this woman with her helplessly clenched and stubborn mind, so though it was a demanding part I didn't struggle with it. Except there was one line I didn't understand, but when I went to John for help he said "If you don't understand why she says it I can't help you." So I slunk away abashed and just said it straight. Not that John was dismissive, he was warm and encouraging throughout and gave me a lovely amber necklace. He was afraid his mother would recognise herself, he said. (One advantage of being old is that you can reveal things like that knowing there's no-one left that might be hurt.) Chris Morahan's still alive – and well I hope – but I don't suppose it will hurt him much if I say that though brilliant he was a bit of a bugger to work with. Well, he reduced both Judi and me to tears and we're pretty tough cookies.

What did I do next? Rode high on the glory for a while I daresay and it was round about then I did another play at the Royal Court. More game-playing. "All chant the lines after each other. All play each others' parts." Jack Shepherd had to meet me in the street and exchange a passing word. He stopped me dead in my path and eyed me intensely, first up and down and then sideways. When I asked him what he was up to he said that his character had been used to thinking of my character cerebrally and was now thinking of her sexually, which meant horizontally. Was he having me on, or could he have meant it? I wish I could believe not, but a whole lot of ridiculous flummery went on in that production. A sweet director but not entirely of this world. It was quite a good play by David Cregan but it was so tarted up in production that it rather missed its mark. We sang some of the dialogue, as I remember, and clod-hopped about a bit. We also pushed the scenery round, for which our Equity Deputy got us nine pounds extra.

I nearly got into a musical after this. I went to see a director I'd worked with (I can never remember directors' names, perhaps *that's* why I'm not a star) about the part of Mme. Defarge, the guillotine-watching tricoteuse in "Two Cities" as they called it. "Can you sing?" he asked. "Well, sort of point numbers, that sort of thing." "That might do," he said. (He'd liked me in the earlier job.) "Come back and do an audition in a month." So I put a panic call in to my agent for a singing teacher and bashed away earnestly with him and at home. At the end of the month my voice was at least stronger if not sweeter. "You'd better have one last lesson the morning of your audition," my teacher said, and worked me so hard my voice disappeared. "You'll be alright it's just nerves," he said. "Here, have these lozenges, it'll come back." It did but not much and before I was half way through my number, trying to compensate with rather a lot of acting, the director leapt onto the stage and put his arm round my shoulders with, instead of the usual "Thanks very much, we'll let you know," a good honest "Sorry, your voice isn't good enough." Nevertheless I kept up the lessons for a while, thinking they might eventually pay off, and I certainly learnt to produce quite a loud sound, though over a rather limited range. In fact I have sung several times since and it seems to be conceded that what I lack in tone I make up for in interpretation. I actually got £6 extra for singing a lullaby in a radio production of "The Dybbuk," another of my Jewish roles.

That wasn't my only disastrous audition. Years earlier, when I was in rep at Westcliffe, a woman rang from London, introducing herself as an agent and saying she could fix an audition for me with Tennents, who were going to produce a double bill of a Greek tragedy and a Restoration comedy. Olivier had just done something like this at the Old Vic and as I was naturally keen to get in on this classy sort of work, I agreed to go up to the Globe Theatre the next afternoon and show casting agent Daphne Rye what I could do. I found "Medea" in the local library and sat up most of the night mugging up a speech which began, "Woe, woe, woe!" and went on to talk about plunging the whetted knife into my children's hearts. I also worked out a few gestures based on pictures on Greek vases. I rather neglected the waggish epilogue I'd chosen to show my Restoration style as I felt this was more up my alley. The morning's rehearsal seemed to go on for ever, and I only just caught the London train. I got to the Globe panting and dishevelled just in time to be announced by the stage manager and told I was on. I took a deep breath, strode to the centre of the stage, flung out my arms and gave my "Woe, woe, woe!" Two cleaning ladies in the dress circle stopped work in alarm and remained transfixed. I ranted on, down on my knees, clutching my brow, doing all I'd practiced in my digs, only louder. There was a pause when I finished, then "Thank you," said Miss Rye in a rather shaken voice. "Yes…well. Thank you." "There's the other piece," I said. "Okay?" and I advanced down front, wagged my finger at her and gave her my Restoration epilogue. The cleaners resumed work and Daphne heard me out, then "Thank you," she said again, "That was very interesting." Feeling wrung out but mildly triumphant, I waited while the stage manager introduced the next actor then asked her eagerly which plays they were doing. "It's for the tour of "The Happiest Days of Your Life" she said. I never heard any more from the mysterious woman who'd rung me.

Auditions are ridiculous things anyway. It's not that I think casting is easy, it's not; and if you get it wrong it's at worst impossible and at best extremely painful to put right. But you can make whopping mistakes however you go about casting, and it would be nice to think it could be achieved without so much trauma and disappointment for actors. But perhaps I'm agonising unnecessarily; perhaps there are actors who actually enjoy auditions. I've just never met one. I may be over-reacting, because when I was running my rep companies I found my casting was continually letting me down. There's one particular incident which is burnt into my soul. It was in the first company I ran, at Eastbourne, and I'd engaged a good-looking, very pleasant leading man. In the first play he seemed a bit weak but as I was acting, directing and generally out of my mind with organizing the start of the season, I didn't let myself worry about it too much. I wasn't in the second play so I saw him from the front, and he just couldn't do it. Every time he had a scene the play was on the floor. I was in despair but I felt I couldn't possibly carry him. So I agonised over it all night, then gritted my teeth, asked him to come and see me, and sacked him. I can't remember how I put it, though I can remember exactly where we were sitting, side by side in the stalls; I can see the upholstery on the seat in front of me that I stared at in horror as he begged me to keep him on for smaller parts as he'd told all his friends of his new job and a lot of them were coming down to see him. I said no, I was sorry, it was all my fault. I'd made a mistake, but I couldn't afford to keep him on for small parts. He said he'd take less money; I said no, it was no good, it wouldn't work. He said he understood; he was sorry he'd let me down. I said – "Oh please! No don't! I'm sorry." I don't know how it ended but I know he continued to take it well and I know I've continued to feel bad about it to this day. Perhaps I should have kept him on? People are more important than plays, but it was my first season and I was desperate to get it right. I wonder if writing it down has exorcised it? It doesn't prove any particular point as I can't remember whether I auditioned him or not.

Chapter 11

One job that didn't involve auditions or reading or even a chat was the Actors Company. Someone in the company who knew you was deputed to ring you up and ask you to join. That made you feel good from the start and the good feeling was nurtured by a deliberate policy of equality, openness, enthusiasm, adventure and – not to sound too corny – love. We really did love one another. I don't think I'm kidding myself, there was during those first seasons, a palpable feeling of goodwill, generosity, co-operation and shared purpose. When I say first seasons it sounds as if I'm going to say it all went wrong, but it didn't. It changed course – what doesn't – but when it drifted into something less ambitious and more conventional it did so without rancour or sense of betrayal.

It was Ian McKellen's brainchild. Well perhaps his and Edward Petherbridge's. Ian had done a two-hander at the Edinburgh Festival and Ted had supported him in a small part, or perhaps it was the other way round, and they both had realised the delight and value of having a supporting part played by a first class actor. So they conceived the idea of setting up a short season of three plays in which all parts would be played by, well – stars, you might say. By the time I joined, the plan had got rather less ambitious, but we were by no means an inconsiderable crew. In alphabetical order we were: Caroline Blakistone, Marian Diamond, Robert Eddison, Tenniel Evans, Felicity Kendal, Matthew Long, Margery Mason, Ian McKellen, Frank Middlemass, Edward Petherbridge,

Moira Redmond, Sheila Reid, Jack Shepherd, Ronnie Stewart and John Tordoff.

The plays had been decided by the time I joined so I don't know how they were chosen, but it can't have been an easy job to accommodate sixteen actors, all having been promised at least one good part. Of course it didn't work perfectly and in fact in the first three plays Ian was the only actor to play two zonking leads, but at least this decision was taken democratically and he was after all the best one for the parts, and certainly the one to bring an audience in.

We opened with a Feydeau farce called "Ruling the Roost", followed it with Ford's "'Tis Pity She's a Whore", and then "The Three Arrows", a new play by Iris Murdoch, set in mediaeval Japan. The company was at first under the aegis of the Cambridge Theatre Company, and Richard Cottrell, its artistic director, directed our first play.

I can't exaggerate the feeling of goodwill and enthusiasm which filled those first meetings, before we even started rehearsals. Ian was obviously anxious not to exploit his position as originator and leader, and continually asked our opinions and judgements. I was impressed by his reaction when I spoke up. He'd shown us a long press release he'd written and I took against it because it featured all the luminaries he'd hoped to get, with scarcely a mention of the B lot he'd landed up with. He immediately thanked me for pointing this out and rewrote it. I think he was desperately anxious not to behave like a star, which wasn't easy because he obviously was one.

It would be fascinating to know why some of us joined. Frank Middlemass for instance, and Robert Eddison, both of whom loyally attended every one of our practically daily meetings but scarcely ever spoke and obviously just wanted to get on with their acting. They were great people to have in the company but it seemed surprising they should be willing to work for £50 a week with no billing or star dressing-rooms or personal publicity or any of the trimmings they must have been used to. Of course I'd found it very seductive to be actually asked out of the blue to join a company, and such an adventurous new one, so perhaps they did too.

Casting had been done before I joined but I was quite happy with two middling good parts and one delicious tiny one in the Feydeau. Ian's bit was tiny too, and my God, did he make something of it! There was a wonderful bit of coat business. Ted too was magic as a hotel manager with a clipboard and a pencil with a life of its own. We opened at Billingham, where they built our scenery, and realised we'd made our first mistake when one set was flesh pink and the actors' faces disappeared. It was hurriedly darkened down for the next performance. We were learning.

As well as choosing plays we chose directors, and I think we may have missed a trick there. Not in our directors, who were all first class, but in the way we worked with them. Mightn't we perhaps have pre-empted the new-style companies which emerged in the ensuing years? Companies like Joint Stock, Paines Plough, Shared Experience, who've developed styles of their own which I feel is the result of the actors being involved in the whole production and not just their own parts. We were a co-op as a company but not to the same extent in our work. David Giles was the first director we actually chose, Richard Cottrell having been gladly accepted as part of the deal with Cambridge. David's an actors' director, creating the sort of warm, encouraging atmosphere actors blossom in. The company loved him and worked with a will to achieve a stylish, full-blooded production of "'Tis Pity She's A Whore". The Iris Murdoch play which followed was strange and fascinating. Was it perhaps the first one written for the stage and not adapted from a novel? I have a feeling it didn't quite work, though Marian Diamond was a beautiful heroine and we did a reasonable job on it. I can't remember much about it except that I opened the play with the line "He must die!" I was a murderous old Japanese nun with a shaved head and Frank Middlemass helped me with my make-up. Iris sat in on rehearsals and was girlishly enthusiastic. "Oh I do think you're all smashing!" Very endearing.

I think the first idea had been for only a short season, after which those among us who could command better paid jobs would go and do them, returning perhaps for a later clutch of plays, but we were all so heady with our unwonted sense of being in control, with a chance to plan our own futures, that we decided to cut ourselves off from Cambridge and set up a permanent company, hopefully with an eventual London home. The Arts Council then took us under its wing and practically every minute not spent on stage was devoted to meetings in which we thrashed out our constitution, policy and future programme.

We lost some of our members after our first short season. Felicity Kendal retired to give birth to a beautiful baby, which was a relief to us all, since her part in "'Tis Pity" had involved tight lacing and being violently thrown about by Ted. Jack Shepherd left too, possibly because the company wasn't as radical as he thought it should be, and Moira, Frank and Ronnie all went on to other things. They were replaced by Sharon Duce, Paola Dionisotti, John Bennett, Ronnie Radd, John Mereno and John Woodvine. We also engaged an organiser and sorely tried company manager, Clare Fox.

We kept the Feydeau and "'Tis Pity" in our repertoire and added "The Wood Demon", Chekov's first version of "Uncle Vanya". Not such a subtle, mature play but with compensating freshness, and giving, in a dinner party scene, a marvellous opportunity for ensemble work. David did a great job, especially in that scene, and the play was generally conceded to be the best thing we'd done so far. We now had three good shows and needed somewhere to play them. We were booked for the Edinburgh Festival and needed to do a certain amount of touring to earn our Arts Council grant, but all the time we were busily searching for a permanent home, in, near or within striking distance of London or – as we got more desperate – anywhere that looked as if it could provide an audience.

In the meantime we fixed a ten weeks' season at the Wimbledon Theatre to be followed by six weeks at the Brooklyn Academy of Music and the Arts. New York! Not exactly Broadway, but still! Waiting for that adventure, we were very happy at Wimbledon. I think it was during this time that I made a serious error of judgement, and said I wasn't interested in being part of this project that Ted Petherbridge was dreaming up. This was a staged version of "Knots", the psychiatrist R. D. Laing's collection of trendy, way-out duologues. I'd met Laing once at a party, where he lay on the floor, replying with shrugs or monosyllables to anyone's attempt at conversation, and then, refusing food or drink, took himself off. So I looked with a jaundiced eye at his slim volume and didn't see how it could possibly work on the stage. It did. My God it did. Ted did a most entertaining, inventive treatment and the company revelled in it. The only longueur for me was Ted's mime act, but then white-faced mime masks and puppets are all things I've given up hope of liking. When the piece was obviously a success, Ted very generously offered to find a slot for me as a raddled singer but I didn't think I'd be good in it or that it would fit into the show. I wish I'd been less blinkered and able to see the piece's potential as I think it was in fact one of the most interesting things the company did, and perhaps showed what our set-up could achieve at its best.

By the Wimbledon season, in Spring 1974, we had five plays in our repertoire, having added "King Lear" and "The Way of the World", both directed by David William. The choice of Lear was partly influenced by our wish to show our regard and admiration for Robert Eddison, and he repaid us with a performance that was of course beautifully spoken and heartbreaking in the later scenes, though one critic's verdict that he was more a willow than an oak was probably justified. As Edgar, Ian went to town in the Poor Tom scenes, threading thorns through his arms, or at least seeming to, and playing one scene completely naked. This was a bit before full frontal male nudity was in fashion, but Wimbledon took it in their stride, though one matinée lady gave voice to an appreciative "Ooh, nice one, Cyril!" Ted was a wonderful stand-up comic as the Fool and I played Old Man.

"The Way of the World" saw our first open competition in the field of casting, as naturally all the women wanted to play Millament. There may have been jockeying for parts in the past but now it was serious. The simple solution was to let David cast it as he saw fit, but we had a half-formulated idea that we could do things more democratically. Of course it was cast by David eventually but the earnest concern that no-one should feel slighted may have helped because I don't remember any bitterness. It's equally possible that I just didn't notice any undercurrents, then or at any other time, since though I was often at loggerheads with Ted, who I thought monopolised the meetings, occasionally crossed swords with Jack, whose didacticism matched my own, and was one of the very few who ever criticised Ian, I was never worried about casting, knowing I'd inevitably play the oldest woman in the play.

With "The Way of the World" I was in luck, as this was Lady Wishfort. I struggled a bit during rehearsals, because David saw her as grotesque, ugly and nasty, and though of course she should be all those things, I wanted to bring out the innocent idiocy of her, which I knew would make it easier to get my precious laughs. David's picture predominated in the first scene, which I played with my hair in curling rags and bursting out of my corsets in all directions. I think even he found this too obscene at dress rehearsal, and a diaphanous wrap was added. It took me a while to marry his conception with mine and I was never as good as I'd hoped to be in the part. I got the laughs all right but I think it was flashy stuff, playing each scene for what it was worth but never quite creating a real woman behind it all. Perhaps it's true, what I've been unwilling to accept, that weekly rep teaches you to play parts off the top of your head. I have a very sharp dramatic instinct that makes me feel I know how to play a part almost as soon as I've read it, but I can see this has dangers. Believe it or not, I think I'm improving.

Next thing, – New York! Surprisingly enough, half of us had never been to America so there was quite a fizz of excitement. Most of us rushed straight from Kennedy Airport up the Empire State Building, unabashed sightseers! Later we did the more conventional theatrical things, supper at Sardi's after our first night (nobody noticed), tea at the Russian Tearooms and so on. The media were really only interested in Ian but he resolutely redirected them to the rest of us, which they glumly accepted. The Brooklyn Academy was running a British season and the Young Vic and the RSC had preceded our six weeks. We saw the RSC's "Richard II" and were able to observe the American custom of applauding after each scene, and even sometimes after a long speech. I found this a bit naff, but when we came to do our own shows we started to expect it, and panic set in if it wasn't forthcoming. "Oh my God! Don't they like it?"

Then disaster struck. The sets and costumes for all our plays had been sent way in advance by sea but where were they? As our opening night drew near, the cables, phone calls and expostulations grew more and more frantic, until, on the day before we were due to open with "Lear", we heard that the ship was still at sea, with no hope of berthing for two more days. I can remember the desperate company meeting, which for some reason took place in the car park. What were our options? Cancel the performance? Dismissed nem con. Hire from local costumiers? No time and too dear. Borrow from the RSC? Wrong period and it would look ridiculous, some in costume and some not. Bare stage, jeans and jumpers and long dresses? Agreed. Someone would have to make a speech and I was given the job, since my part of Old Man gave me plenty of time to compose one. After a restless night I'd decided that the situation needed more than just a report and plea for indulgence, so I rather went to town, starting with a brief account of how the Actors Company worked and going on to expatiate at some length on the business of deciding on style, choosing designers and creating from their designs, before I revealed that the result of all this was on the high seas and they weren't going to see any of it. I got a few good laughs and even some of those rounds of applause I'd been so snooty about, and the play certainly got a warm reception. The publicity did us no harm either. All our stuff arrived the next day but the company felt time was needed to get it in order, and asked me to make my speech again. But I thought we should have buckled to, ironed our own dresses, sorted out our own props and given as near a proper show as we could, so I refused and Ian did it. He didn't get my laughs though.

I'm not sure who fixed our digs in Manhattan but I was lucky enough to be put in the famous Chelsea Hotel, erstwhile haunt of Hemingway, Brendan Behan and other cult figures. The funny little foyer was crammed with bits of esoteric art in various stages of decay, perhaps offered in lieu of rent, and the apartments were pretty crummy, but after all, this was Greenwich Village, and Washington Square was just round the corner. Marian Diamond and I shared an apartment for a couple of weeks, until the cockroaches and mice got her down and she moved in with friends. I found the place mysteriously congenial, though the cooker, fridge and shower only worked now and then. Some people had lived there for years, and once or twice I was invited into apartments crammed with mementoes and once so smothered with climbing plants there was practically no daylight. As if to confirm the hotel's la vie bohème credentials, the body of a suicide was carried through the foyer while I was paying my bill. The management only shrugged a resigned apology.

I hadn't liked New York when I'd been there before, in fine weather and staying in Park Avenue, and now it was bitterly cold, with black snow piled on the sidewalks, and though I was relishing the whole experience I couldn't share the company's enthusiasm for the Big Apple. I had the heretical conviction that it was much slower than London, and as for Central Park, well really! Hemmed in by skyscrapers, no hope of forgetting you're in the middle of a city. The derelicts sleeping over heating outlets and the misfits at street corners hurling obscenities were upsetting too. We hadn't got used to people sleeping in doorways at that time. The subway journey to and from Brooklyn was supposed to be dangerous and many of the company took cabs but either from meanness or a determination to see New York as it really was, I persevered. The most frightening thing about it was the heavily armed police, otherwise it seemed to be used mainly by people staring gloomily into space or muttering to themselves. When it wasn't too cold and we didn't have a meeting I'd go and sit in Washington Square, where people played volleyball and chess and seemed more friendly. Once an old man came and sat beside me on a wall and said I reminded him of Edna St. Vincent Millay, who often used to sit just there. "I burn my candle at both ends," I remarked. "It will not last the night," he replied. "But ah my foes and oh my friends," (together) "It gives a lovely light!" Then we went somewhere warmer to discuss Millay over a coffee. I was a great fan at the time, and still am in a modified way.

Then someone, Ian I suppose, got us an invitation to sit in on a session of the Actors' Studio. This turned out to be quite a shock. We'd all gone along excited at the prospect of seeing the famous Method in operation but what we saw was a rehearsal in front of a largish audience, so that we weren't sure if we were seeing a genuine workout. But surely this wasn't the Method? It seemed like the most conventional old fashioned type of rehearsal, with the director, Elia Kazan no less, continually pulling the actors up, correcting them and seemingly deliberately destroying their confidence. Our company was introduced at the end and asked for comment, as they'd been doing Shakespeare. There was a pretty ghastly pause, which Ian and even Ted failed to break, so I stammered out something about the metre being an aid to inter-pretation. To my horror Kazan asked if I would be prepared to give some help in this area; if so, students could contact me in the coffee bar. Several spoke to me but only one signed up and we arranged for him to come to the Chelsea next day.

He was a handsome black man in his thirties and he arrived carrying a recorder, the purpose of which was revealed when he said he was doing the first speech in "Richard III", with its reference to "the piping times of peace." He'd been working on just that speech, he said, not the whole part, for two months, and was due to deliver it next week. He didn't seem to have any plan to actually play the recorder, just to wave it about at the appropriate line. I was flummoxed. Where could I start? We had three sessions and talked about the part and the verse and acting and life in general and got on very well, but of course it made no impression on his performance. He asked me to attend his audition and it was grim. It wasn't just that he was torn to pieces; before he did his bit I had to sit through a whole lot of other auditions, including Desdemona's death scene. This started with her playing with a doll, cuddling it, feeding it, shaking it and finally taking it to bed with her and falling asleep. Enter Othello, who addressed a carpet hanging on the back wall with a long African chant before getting down to "It is the cause." I don't know at which point that scene finished but the afternoon went on for ever, with each offering subjected to comment, usually scathing, from the floor as well as Kazan. I couldn't face my pupil and crept away after he'd been demolished. Was this the studio that had produced Brando, Steiger and all those other impressive actors? I was totally bewildered and fell back on by my old suspicion that actors are born not made, and that Americans are addicted to studying their navels.

I'm not sure what we did when we came back. I know I took the rehearsals which put some new people in "Lear" and I also directed a nice little lunch hour play we did at the Mermaid. It was a year or so before I rejoined the company for a British and Scandinavian tour. It was less star-studded now and had lost some of its pioneering spirit, though still committed to democratic principles. I was the only "founder member" and swanned into the first meeting with cries of joy, dispensing hugs and kisses as had been our wont, to find the rest of the cast a little startled at such OTT behaviour. We were to do Osborne's "The Entertainer" and Pinero's "The Amazons", a jokey sort of feminist play. The Arts

Council was still backing us, though rather less enthusiastically, but that was all to the good as it meant we were playing universities and studio theatres instead of the great barns the original company had been condemned to.

The sea was frozen in Finland but the native actors gave us a warm welcome into their theatres, which were a revelation to British actors, used to carpets one side of the passdoor and bare boards the other. Here there were saunas and spacious rest rooms and restaurants serving hot meals all day. All Scandinavian theatres seem to house permanent companies so the actors use the backstage facilities if they're in the current play or not. No bars though. Drunkenness seems to be the only reason an actor can lose his otherwise assured job for life. Professional theatre was fairly recent in Finland at that time but there had always been lots of amateur companies. "Everyone has always acted" we were told, and certainly they seemed completely and happily at home on the stage. I saw three plays without understanding a word, but you couldn't be bored. The acting was so natural and spirited that you found yourself laughing, clapping and feeling you understood the whole thing. They didn't seem to need an Actor's Studio to "release" them.

In Helsinki we stayed in the YMCA, where my bedside table held a bible and a hard core porn mag. Some of us went for a sauna, half-hoping, half-fearing we'd be rolled in the snow and beaten with birch twigs, but it was just very smart and conventional and the pool was lukewarm. One of our actors had an international gay guide which recommended Helsinki Park as *the* cruising area. He came back from a tentative foray in the driving snow and icy wind saying Finnish gays must be very tough or very desperate. We found Helsinki a smart, sophisticated town but I think we all preferred Oulu, which we reached by coach, seeing nothing on the road for hours but frozen lakes, fir forests and here and there a wooden house, a reindeer or another car. Finland did seem a very empty country and Oulu a long way from anywhere so perhaps it wasn't surprising we were received so joyously and made such a fuss of. Our visit meant the resident actors were on holiday, so they wanted to whoop it up with us night after night. Sue Edmonstone, one of our more glamorous girls, was doggedly pursued by one actor with a plaintive cry of

"The Pulpit" Norway. Ragnar is a bit lower down!

"But where is long tall Sue?" On the coach back to Helsinki she confessed to feeling terribly sorry for him because he'd turned up at her room the night before and she'd had to be quite harsh to get rid of him. She didn't understand why this was greeted with roars of laughter until we revealed that he'd turned up at the bedroom of every single female, getting more and more drunk with each visit. I must have been the last because I had no difficulty pushing him through the door, after which there was a loud thump.

Did you know there are more pigs than people in Denmark? We never saw one though; they're all under cover in the winter. We only played Copenhagen but we took a trip out to Elsinore and one of our actors, who was going to play Hamlet in New Zealand, got in a photo op on the battlements. The castle wasn't all that impressive but the Royal Palace in Copenhagen was elegant, and the grounds were open to the public, which seemed nice and democratic. We didn't see any Royals on bikes though.

Oslo was impressive. Lots of art in the parks and galleries, not just Munch, quite cheerful stuff. Then Stavanger, a bustling port. More of the friendly actors, one of whom bought a huge bag of prawns in the harbour, added a couple of bottles of wine and took some of us for a picnic on a nearby hill. We were just getting down to it when a police car screeched to a halt. Someone had reported there were people drinking liquor in the open air. Our Norwegian friend saved us from arrest and we slunk off to continue the party in the hotel. On the last day an actor and his artist-teacher wife invited some of us to lunch and we had a sumptuous meal in their typical Norwegian house right on a fjord. Gunwar and Ragnar are now my valued friends and we've stayed in each others' homes many times. I swam in their icy fjord and Ragnar took me on a seven hour there and back climb when I stayed with them, but they trumped my ace by seeing nine plays in their one week in London.

Chapter 12

My Hampstead pad, which I sometimes think is my most precious possession, has served me well not only as a home but a provider of friends. Since there's more than enough room for me in the garden flat, I've let the first floor rooms to various people over the years. At first I thought – this was in the fifties – it would be fun to put cards in newsagents' windows saying "Any colour welcome, even white" and I had Indian, Nigerian, Jamaican and Chinese tenants, some fine, some a bit dodgy. One very nice Nigerian girl with a beautiful fat baby could never quite believe that it wasn't all right to light a fire in the passage for her cooking. It did no real harm to the tiled floor but it set the smoke alarm off. Then I had some Indians who sublet the rooms to their nightworker friends in the daytime, and two Chinese waiters who knocked off work at 2 am and brought their friends home for a party. So I got more choosy, and struck lucky with young American academics. First a laid-back Californian couple, he ostensibly working on his PHD, she taking a year or so off, both mainly occupied in transcendental meditation. (When I later stayed with him and his second wife in Los Angeles he was meditating five hours a day and claimed to be levitating. But no, he said, sorry, it didn't work with anyone else in the room. They were perfect tenants, very quiet of course, but interesting too. I even had a go at TM under their influence. My niece Stephanie, Grace's daughter, who was sharing the ground floor with them, and I went along to a few classes and finally our individual inaugurations.

We each had to take along three pieces of fruit, some flowers and a clean white handkerchief. There was a picture of the Maharishi with a votive light and various flowers and icons about. I really can't remember what I had to do except give up all but one piece of fruit and take some sort of vow. Then I was given my dead-secret personal mantra, which must never be divulged to a living soul and which I must chant, either softly or in my head, to help my meditation. Since I was paying for all this and fancied a bit more heightened consciousness, à la LSD, I tried very hard to take it seriously. I wasn't helped by Steph, who emerged giggling and with the muttered comment that they'd never be short of fruit. Still, we persevered for about a month, religiously meditating twice a day, though Steph complained that she kept falling asleep. Then one day she unthinkingly said "I feel so silly, sitting there cross-legged saying Shyam," "Saying what!" "Oh my God, I've said it. Will that break the spell or something?" "But that's *my* mantra!" "Well it's mine too." We somehow lost our faith then. And as far as I know no-one's ever *seen* anyone levitating. Then that couple went off back to California, where I expect he's still working on his PHD, and after a while their place was taken by Linda and Peter Parshall, another couple of American academics, who've been my great friends for the last 40 odd years.

It was Linda who launched me on my academic career. The professor who was running the Summer School at her university in Portland, Oregon decided he wanted to pep up the operation with a few star performers from abroad. "I know a star!" said Linda, and persuaded me to send in my curriculum vitae. It seemed a strange term to apply to my erratic career, but I duly wrote up an account of my activities, which looked unexpectedly impressive on paper, and was hired. What did I propose to teach, they asked. Resisting the urge to reply "God alone knows" I dredged up the idea of taking a topical issue, researching it, and creating a short play on the subject. This was at the time when the murderer Gary Gilmore was demanding to be executed rather than imprisoned and I thought we might do something on that.

But how? How did you get people to improvise? If only I'd been to drama school. I decided to ask Anna Sher, who does marvels with working class kids, if I could sit in on a class. I was impressed and intimidated in equal parts, and, though I doubted if I could imitate her, I bought her record and booklet as a lifeline in case of need. I wasn't reassured by receiving the prospectus for the Summer School, which listed me as teaching Creative Reality Theater. Still, I thought, it's only a three week course and then Linda and Peter and I are off to Hawaii.

I was very kindly received at Portland State University, together with my fellow "star", an ex-member of the British Secret Service. I was relieved that the press were more interested in him, an actual spy, than in me, as I was still flummoxed when asked to define "creative reality theater". When it came to the classes I realised I'd been right to be scared; I wasn't any good at inspiring and guiding improvisation. Linda, guiltily responding to my "You got me into this!" worked with me night after night devising extensive scenarios crammed with colourful characters. Next day the students would polish them off and be ready for the next one in a matter of minutes. Then I tried asking them to act a scene to link first and last lines – "I had this awful toothache . . . . . I didn't know he was married." – that sort of thing. They got through that in two minutes flat. Except for one girl, or rather a woman in her thirties, who did every improvisation kneeling by her mother's gravestone. "Oh Mom," she'd address the chair she'd set up, "I had this awful toothache. But Mom, if you'd just listen to me. I know I haven't been much of a daughter but listen Mom – " and then it would all pour out; riveting stuff, some of it, but showing no signs of stopping or reaching the punch line. Deciding that perhaps therapy went with the job, I got her on her own and asked sympathetically when exactly her mother had died. "Oh, Mom's not dead," she said. "Oh gee no, mom's very much alive."

I only had nine in my class; two drama teachers (Oh God!) five students and two ladies in their seventies. Eventually we decided we'd do not a play but a series of sketches, songs and monologues.

Abandoning with relief our exercises in relaxation, inter-relating, trust-establishing and the like, we settled down to decide on a theme. Almost unanimously they plumped for death. Death as the Last Taboo, "We could call it 'Death is a Four Letter Word'" someone said, and just stopping myself from being naff enough to say "But it's not" I agreed and we went into production. Then things started to happen. Now that I'd released control, people blossomed. Songs and poems were written, sketches improvised and scripted, skits on tv shows worked up. It was just a question of whipping them into shape and tying them together. It was a scramble getting it ready on time and I lost my hard-earned cool and shouted a bit, but eventually we got it on for a lunchtime performance on the campus and it went over quite well.

The hit of the show was unquestionably the two old ladies, who devised a sketch where they went to a mortician's, trying on their "caskets". "I always wanted to be married in pink," one said. "Well nobody asked me, but I'm going to be buried in it. What do you think? Does it suit me?" The fact that they were the genuine article gave it a real frisson, and the youthful audience loved it. The cast seemed to have enjoyed themselves finally and said they'd learned a lot. I had too, mostly about drawing things from people instead of imposing my own ideas. I wouldn't say the lesson has stuck. I'll never be able to accept, as I suppose one should in academic work, that it's the process not the product that matters. I can't bear the show not to be as good as possible. Anyway, after a blissful interlude in Hawaii I began to think perhaps it hadn't been such a trauma and I might do it again. I toyed with the idea of circulating my impressive cv round the American academic scene but then some nice acting jobs turned up and I settled for what I more or less knew I could do.

So it was ten years before I returned to American academe, this time to Gustavos Adolphus College in Minnesota, where my nephew Gregory, Bert's son, was teaching. Sounds like nepotism but in fact Rob Gardner, the college's drama teacher, had seen me in London, and the RSC probably has a certain cachet in mid west

America. This time I was to teach half a semester, six weeks, and I was told I could do anything I liked. Why didn't I choose just to direct a play? Why do I have to put myself through these agonies? I suppose I thought it would be easier this time. I knew the pitfalls and anyway I was to have an assistant; she could take all those warming-up exercises I could never make myself see the point of. I also knew a little more, or thought I did, of improvising techniques, having been to a few classes, read a lot of books and picked a few friends' brains. So I said I'd do my "creative reality" bit again. Rob was directing "Romeo and Juliet" at the same time as my rehearsals so the more ambitious of the students had joined his cast, and as I refused to hold auditions and threw my course open to anyone who wanted to come along, I got mainly beginners, eight girls and five boys. I had an initial advantage in having played the Ancient Booer in "The Princess Bride", a cult film on the American campuses, so they saw me as a genuine star, and I could sometimes defuse tricky moments with a well timed "Boo!" I'd read a book about Mike Leigh's methods and thought I might make at least the initial exercise work. This was to ask each actor to come with a list of the most interesting people they knew, then we could choose one for them to base a character on. I duly called all my girls and boys in singly and made this suggestion. One and all told me about their best friend at school. Asked to throw the net wider, some mentioned their parents. All right, what were they interested in? What got them excited? Sport. Pop stars. Time was getting on so I threw my principles to the wind and started feeding in subjects I was interested in.

Quite soon it was agreed we'd do a play about abortion, with homosexuality as a sub-plot. Rob may have been startled but took it calmly, and Jo, the young drama teacher who'd agreed to help me, was unfazed.

Discussions were quite lively now, but when I tried to translate them into improvisations from which I could fashion a script, chaos ensued. No matter how I tried to structure the sessions, nothing of use emerged. Panicking, and convinced I'd never master this technique, I did my second cop-out and decided to write the play by myself. So from then on I got up at 7, swam in their wonderful deserted pool, wrote from 8 to 4, put it on tape to be typed, had a game of tennis with Greg and got to know his wife and kids, and rehearsed from 7 to 10. If this sounds ordered and relaxed, I can only say I was in a state of frenzy throughout. This was an altogether more ambitious project than the larky programme we'd thrown together and performed free in the open air in Portland. This time we were giving four performances in the college theatre and people were paying. I was just not sure whether I could write a play in three and a half weeks, which was all the time that remained. There was plenty of material to work on. Abortion was a hot issue, then as now, and the dilemma of a student forced to choose between keeping either her baby or her place at college, had been faced a year ago in this very school. Feelings pro and con ran high among my students and gave me good hints for casting. I didn't want the pregnant girl to be a pathetic little waif, so I cast our one fat girl in the part. She'd never acted before but was eager to learn, grew in confidence under one's eyes and eventually made a fine pivot for the play and didn't mind at all, in fact encouraged the jokes about her weight. The homosexual sub-plot didn't grab the cast to the same degree. In fact it was probably only in the play because I wanted to bang that particular drum. I suspected that a couple of my actors were in fact gay but since they were most decidedly not out it didn't seem fair to cast either of them as the super-sportsman and darling of the girls who finally found the courage to declare himself. We had one lad who was perfect for the part though, a typical jock to whom all girls were chicks and all gays pouffs. As the script only arrived day by day no-one knew quite how the characters were going to develop, and though the girls soon began to guess and giggle, it was not until the final scene was in his hand that he realised he was playing "one of them". He took it well though – "Just so long as people don't think I really am" – and handled his coming-out scene with aplomb.

It looked as if the play wouldn't run much more than an hour so I said we should invite people for a discussion afterwards. It never worked, Jo said. People didn't stay and if they did they didn't talk. At the most we could try it for one night. I dug my heels in. "They'll talk about this." I said, "We'll put it on the posters and we'll have it every night." Everybody stayed and you couldn't stop them talking. A respectable middle-aged lady stood up and spoke of the horror of her illegal abortion, adopted children praised their natural mothers for having them, the girl who'd had to leave the college when she was pregnant turned up with her baby, and though she didn't speak, her friends did, to say that if she'd fought like the girl in the play she might not have had to leave. It wasn't so easy to get people talking about homosexuality, which they seemed to think had nothing to do with them. The leader of the very small gay group in the college spoke up, and I stoked that fire as much as I could but it didn't really ignite. It's a Lutheran college and though that creed seems pleasantly liberal after Catholicism I suppose it has its limits. On second thoughts, not really. At the end of show party which Greg and Ruth gave me the college pastor told me quietly that before abortion was legalised in Minnesota a chain of Lutheran ministers ran a grapevine getting young girls to California for their terminations. America never stops surprising you.

Martin, a young Swedish teacher who'd sat in on some of my rehearsals, was keen for me to do something at the Mora Folkhogskola where he taught. I agreed, as I always do to most things, then forgot all about it, so it was a bit of a facer when a couple of years later he rang and said how about it and would I come and teach the special Spring session for the whole of May? I'd just arranged to go to Birmingham Rep to do a part nothing would have made me give up – going from age 5 to 87 – but we were finishing the last week in April so I said, sure, only this time I won't attempt all that impro stuff. When you've signed them up, get them all to write to me with photos and chats about themselves, and I'll write a play for them before I come out.

The Birmingham play, "My Mother Said I Never Should", was enormous fun but quite demanding, so I couldn't really start writing until we'd opened. In the meantime the photos and lifestories had arrived – ten girls, one woman and one boy. What sort of cast is that? Since some of them claimed to sing or dance and the boy played the guitar I toyed with the idea of a musical but eventually decided I'd write a straight play and if we could find room for songs, well and good.

*Me, aged 5, with Janice Mackenzie, Louise Yates and
Christine Absalom, Birmingham Rep, 1980*

Chapter 13

I wasted the first of my five weeks thrashing about trying to think of a plot to accommodate this ridiculous cast and finally couldn't think any anything better than to set it in the dancing class of a Folk High School and then set the cat among the pigeons by having the boy join the class. A start perhaps but hardly a play. Okay, back to my old mainstay – a pregnant girl. This time she can be clever, career-orientated and opposed equally to abortion and motherhood. Her choice of adoption makes waves, particularly in the family of one of the other girls, herself adopted, who now feels she wants to seek out her natural mother. She does and finds her a hard-faced schemer, so it's back to love and kisses with her adopted mum. (Thank God for my one middle-aged woman.) I struggled with all this, interlaced with comedy of course, and managed to produce a 65-minute script with three days left to type it up, send it off, get my work permit – the Swedish Embassy being polite but mysteriously obstructive – say goodbye to Birmingham and get on the plane.

I was welcomed at the tiny Mora airport by Martin and half my cast. Most of the girls were even prettier than their photos, and Ola, the boy whom I'd written as the dreamboat all the girls were mad about, certainly had a nice face, though it was a pity he was only just over five foot. I'd arrived on the first of May so when we got to the Folk High School we found everyone assembled round a huge bonfire on the lawn, celebrating with songs and speeches, buns and soft drinks. Folk High Schools are a Scandinavian phenomenon and have flourished in the four countries for over a hundred years. Sweden has a hundred and twenty-three of them and though they share a common ethos each school is free to shape its own curriculum, activities and rules of conduct. These are strikingly liberal. The minimum student age is eighteen; there is no maximum. No qualification is demanded for entry, no classes are mandatory and no-one it seems can be chucked out. "Not ever?" I asked. "Well perhaps for persistent drunkenness, but we've never known it." The schools are strictly dry, though I had a little wine at dinner parties and a nightly low alcohol beer with Martin. Students live either in the neighbourhood or in college, sometimes with their children. If girls and boys decide to cohabit they're given a double room. A fair proportion of the students are refugees from conventional education or from dead-end jobs, and the schools also try to make special provision for the psychologically or physically handicapped. Many of the classes are in traditional arts and crafts – woodwork, bark-weaving, leatherwork with reindeer skins, pottery and so on. Among the objectives set out in the Folk High Schools Ordinance are "To increase the student's awareness of his or her own circumstances and those of the world at large, and deepen the student's sensitivity and experiential capacity." One could hardly quarrel with that, so why did I find myself in my room after every rehearsal, grinding my teeth over my duty-free Scotch and muttering about a lot of feather-bedded layabouts? Because I'm an autocrat and a slavedriver or because they hadn't the faintest idea of commitment or self-discipline? Bit of both, obviously, but it was my job to somehow weld the two styles into a working partnership. I didn't succeed. As usual I got on a far better show than there was any right to expect but there were a few fights on the way. My first setback was at the readthrough. One of the cast immediately said we couldn't do the play. Adoption was unknown in Sweden except for refugee children; no-one would believe the story. Fighting my resentment (all those late nights slaving away in Birmingham) I said I couldn't write another play in the time. What did she suggest? Some of the other girls, mainly the ones with leading parts, thought we'd get away with it, so I agreed to see what mitigating factors I could introduce and we got on with the reading. I soon saw, or rather heard, that I'd made a mistake in writing the play in highly colloquial English which not only didn't suit the singsong tune of Swedish voices but was often incomprehensible to the actors. So we continually ironed it out into flat, uncolourful language which I hated but they felt happier with and knew the audience would. We only rehearsed from 8.30 until 2 and it turned out our first performance was at the beginning of the fourth week not the end, so barely controlled despair set in with me as one after another of the girls failed to turn up for rehearsals for what seemed ludicrously inadequate reasons. "Headache! What's wrong with aspirin? Period pains? So what?" Even when one of the girls suffered date rape and had to spend time with the police I couldn't help feeling it was a conspiracy to rob me of rehearsal time. I had to resist an urge to say "Oh darling, how awful, I'm so sorry, but come on dear, we've all been raped in our time, it needn't stop us rehearsing." I had been, in fact, during the War. Thrown off my bike by a G.I. outside Peterborough, threatened with a knife, and then subjected to all sorts of offensive questioning by the military police when I was fool enough to report it. So I should have felt more sympathy, but it was a long time ago and I certainly hadn't been off work. Martin handled the crisis in recognisably Folk High School style. The cast were called together and everyone was encouraged to sympathise and comfort her, and it seemed to help.

Another frustration was that the dancing practice seemed to take an inordinate slice out of my rehearsal time. Asa was doing a great job but did she really have to do all those mood exercises before she got down to work? The dance was to be African, which was Asa's speciality. It seemed a bit repetitive to me but I'd been to a local ballet school display where a large audience seemed quite happy watching girl after girl perform roughly the same steps, so perhaps Swedes didn't bore easily. Martin had warned me before I left England that the three boys and a girl he'd enlisted as stage management might pose a few problems. One was schizophrenic, one had hearing and motor neuron disabilities, one was withdrawn and one subject to mood swings. Working in a team and being entrusted with important jobs was supposed to give them much-needed confidence. Martin doggedly persisted in allotting them tasks and attempting to nurse them through before he took over himself, each time disappointed but undeterred. Fortunately he was very efficient as well as sympathetic over my frustration, though it obviously grieved him that I couldn't relax into the all-understanding, all-tolerant laissez-faire ethos of the place.

The play was to be put on in the gymnasium, but, since I have an implacable objection to an auditorium without a rake, we decided together that we would put the audience on the stage, build further platforms down from it and do the play on the main floor. The resources and co-operative spirit of the school served us well here, and once Martin had accepted that power tools and his crew didn't go together, the platforms were built in no time. Then the walls were draped in African-style painted cloths designed by Martin's artist wife – or rather Britti Halvarsson, Swedish people not going in for marriage in a big way – and the setting at least looked great. At this stage I gave way on a long contested point and agreed to have a prompter sitting in full view of the audience, armed with script and torch and ready to respond to a fluff or a nod from any of the actors. This was absolutely standard they assured me, even at the National Theatre, and they would all go to pieces without it. Reluctantly relinquishing, in the face of my "Don't even think of it!" look, the idea of giving one of his crew a final chance to shine, Martin agreed to take on the job. Some of the girls had thrown temperaments at having to shift the furniture but caved in when I threatened to have the stage-management team do it, and gradually the actors grew into their parts, the dances took shape, the final one, with costumes and drummers, looked like providing a rousing finale, and it seemed the play was as good as we could make it. I had one final clash with members of the cast who wanted to wander the stage during dress rehearsal taking photos, and decided to forget all about it until The Night and take myself off for my daily lifesaver, a swim in one of the lakes.

I'd early established this as an unbreakable routine. There'd been snow in the ditches when I arrived but within a few days the sun had come out and continued to blaze from 4 am to 10 pm for the rest of the month. A kind benefactor had responded to an appeal made by the headmaster and lent me a bike, so I was free to wobble off on the cycle tracks, dismounting when I had to cross the road, to discover icy but swimmable lakes and, as the month progressed, more and more wild flowers, many like the ones at home but much bigger and more profuse. So every morning I strove and fumed and every afternoon I splashed and squealed with joy in the invigoratingly icy water and then lay in the sun wondering why I'd got so het up that morning just because one of the girls had yawned during another one's big speech.

It was a wrench to leave this and get back for the last meal of the day at 4:30, after which the daylight evening stretched out until getting on for midnight. Sometimes I skipped the meal and made do with the goodies I was allowed to plunder from the kitchen store cupboards. The food, which I got free and everybody else paid for, was often very nice indeed, though relentlessly healthy.

Most evenings I'd go down to Martin and Britti, who lived just across the playing field near to the traditional log houses and the lake where they soaked the reindeers' hides before pounding them for leatherwork. I'd watched this activity and hadn't managed to feel that any product warranted such relentless drudgery, but I enjoyed whiling away the long light evenings with Martin and Britti and their fat, laughing baby, sipping our one per cent alcohol and agreeing about politics. They were all such *good* people, those who worked in that place. I got to know a few of the other teachers – not intimately, that's not easy in Sweden – and there was such high moral purpose and charity expressed in all directions. Quite shaming, though it didn't make me noticeably less acerbic. Some of it may have stemmed from the headmaster, or rektor, who was my idea of a saint; that's to say, broadminded, benevolent and funny with it, but I suspect it runs through all the F.H.S. The rektor finally enlightened me as to why the Swedish embassy had been so sticky over my work permit. "Surely you can find a Swedish person to do this work?" they'd protested, and when he disagreed, "But why this woman? She's so *old*. What if she's ill?" "We have reciprocal health services." "But what if she *dies*!" "Then, as a rektor of the Lutheran Church, I will give her a first class funeral." And so I got my permit; but the fact of my advanced age was still felt to be crucial by all the local media. Everything began with "This remarkable 77-year-old woman." I got a bit fed up with it because, though I've no objection to being old or to who knows it, I don't like to think it's my only claim to distinction. My age helps though, when I swim. I've three times won the Women's over-70 group in the National Swimathon, and was once presented with my prize by a startled Bernard Cribbens. He promptly asked me to play in a "celebrities" tennis match, where I didn't do so well.

But back to Rektor Rainer, who's not Swedish, – which I imagine makes it easier to be funny. Shouldn't stereotype of course but in fact most Swedes will claim, not without complacency, to be cool and difficult to know, and they certainly don't go in a lot for giggles. Rainer, though, is a mixture of German, Hungarian and Jew, and maybe a few more, and as unlike a headmaster as one can imagine, wandering around barefoot, driving off alone with a truckful of food and medicines to Estonia, seemingly giving his teachers carte blanche with anything they care to dream up. I think he may be exceptional, even in his setting, because I was often asked proudly "What do you think of our rektor? Isn't he extraordinary!" His wife's by way of being an angel too, but in a more Swedish style.

Our four shows went without disaster – and actually without a single prompt – and the local critics seemed impressed. One of them told me, and to my delight in front of the girl who'd first said we couldn't do the play, that he was particularly interested as he himself was adopted. The company gave me a pottery figure they knew I'd coveted, I said how well they'd all done and we parted in general amity, though without the hugs and protestations that "We must keep up!" you get used to in this country. They sent me a joint Christmas card though, but I expect Martin put them up to it.

Bernard Cribbins, Duncan Goodhew and me with my first prize

Chapter 14

One of the great and glorious perks of being an actor is that you get to go abroad, where you live in a style to which you have otherwise small hope of being accustomed. In fact I've only been on three foreign tours apart from ENSA but they've taken me to fourteen different countries, most of which I'd never have seen under my own steam. The Watford rep took out "The Merchant of Venice" and "Pygmalion", and Arthur Cox, who was playing Doolittle and Gratiano, somehow wangled me into the company. This was particularly magnanimous of Arthur as he'd written to me for a job in Bangor and I hadn't even answered his letter. The only part left for me was Mrs. Eynesford-Hill in "Pygmalion" but the British Council, who were sending the tour out, asked Margaretta Scott and me to do a poetry recital as neither of us was in "The Merchant". Margaretta, who was experienced in this field, contacted a man who arranged a programme for us. It seemed alarmingly highbrow to me, especially for our prospective audiences, mainly schools with English at best the second language. Margaretta was more at home than I with the chunks of Greek drama we hurled at each other but I did my best, and we shared out some of the rest of the programme to taste. The Arts Council booked a tryout for us at the Malayan Institute, whose members were mostly studying engineering, accountancy, business and the like. So one Saturday night (ill-chosen since that's when they're all out on the town) we presented ourselves in our elegant long dresses, clutching our scripts, and on my part at least, distinctly worried. It took a while to muster even a token audience but finally we started. They took the Greek drama on the chin, only one or two melting away from the back rows, and sat more or less attentive while we alternated our pieces, but when it came to our concerted finale, a spirited rendering of Edward Lear's "Pelican Chorus", I think they became convinced they were watching a couple of ancient madwomen. It must have been quite a sight, these two elderly bespectacled women advancing on them with

"Ploffskin, Pluffskin, Pelican jee!
We think no birds so happy as we!
Plumpskin, Ploshkin Pelican jill!
We think so then and we thought so still."

When we finished they sat in complete bemused silence, until our desperate bows released them to clap and depart.

Margaretta and I decided, reasonably amicably, that we'd be better off splitting the recital into individual programmes, so I devised one, not very sensibly really, on the seasons in England. Then, when we got going in India, Margaretta felt, probably quite justifiably, that I was hogging the available time, so we split and halved the dates. I enlarged and revised my programme and it went down quite well, getting a few laughs even with the language difficulty. Eventually we both broadcast our pieces on Radio Malaya. I remember the sound engineer was reading a magazine as I did mine.

Our first call was New Delhi. We were only in India a fortnight and got little chance officially to meet any but the upper crust, British and Indian, but even so it was an overwhelming experience. Not our little world; not the performances or the receptions or the fun in the pool or the excursions; not even the Taj Mahal, just the whole strange, ancient, magnificent, appalling, mysterious country. I did have one or two encounters with ordinary, or extraordinary, Indian people. Once a woman came up and joined me in a café and talked at some length about Indian and Western food, ending up by begging me to allow her to order and pay for the specialities she would most like me to try. My protests not availing, I gratefully accepted. She went off triumphantly and I waited nervously for these exotic delicacies. After forty minutes I realised she wasn't coming back.

On a walk in the country (How did I get there? Perhaps there was a bus) I came across a small ruined temple inhabited by a very ragged and rather dirty old man. I was about to apologise and retreat when he addressed me in fluent English and asked my opinion of Ernest Hemingway. After I'd given it (well not honestly because I actually considered him a bit of a macho posturer) we went on to discuss Joseph Conrad and Jack London and other writers of whom he knew much more than me. I wondered if perhaps he'd been a teacher but no, he said, he had never held any position, nor had he ever married or had a home. He'd learnt English at school and had since spent his time reading it. He found he could live on very little and had been living in the ruined little temple for many years now. When I got up to go – we'd been sitting on the floor of the temple, made long ago of compressed cattle dung but quite clean and sweet – I waited for the request for alms. When it didn't come I offered him what I had but he absolutely refused to take it. He had enjoyed our meeting, he said, and didn't want to spoil it with money. He was barefoot, with long matted hair and beard and wearing only a ragged dhoti. No home, no visible means of support, but a Hemingway buff. Can anyone begin to understand India?

Calcutta was next and somehow more what one expected. Swarms of ragged children at the airport, reputedly brought in from the country by pimps, clutching at your clothes with "Me no father, me no mother!" lepers with begging bowls, whole families living in the dusty streets under trees, emaciated sacred cows blocking the traffic, skeletal rickshaw men said to have a life expectancy of twenty-four, and Mother Theresa's establishment. 'The company was divided about visiting this, some feeling It voyeuristic and others our duty to see it. It was a harrowing experience and at the time I felt only amazement and respect for the dedicated workers, not only those in the religious order but the lay assistants, American, English and Indian. Over the years though I've grown more critical. What sort of creed condemns women to produce babies they have no hope of feeding? The stick-like infants I saw being lovingly coaxed away from death had probably already suffered brain damage, and would face further starvation when they gave way to the next intake. The skeletal men propped against the walls to "die with dignity" would be replaced by more of the same. The children taken in from the streets who clambered over us, desperate for affection, until their hands were prised off, the men and women being taught to walk again, dragging their insect-like limbs along parallel bars, they were all being tirelessly and lovingly nurtured by the workers but no-one was offering any solution or questioning the system which produced these horrors. The only evidence of anything constructive was given by the men and women crouched in the yard, beating away at the coconut fibre shells which kindly people threw into the ditch outside the settlement, work said to be reserved for those who had at least eight people dependent on them, and the tiny amount they got for it largely went to the landlords of the shacks they lived in. We argued about it in the company but not that much. We were having too good a time at the Tolly Gunge Club, with its vast green lawns, tennis courts and gin and tonics by the pool. Still, as we weren't allowed to take money out of India, we all put our rupees into the Mother Theresa box at the airport, after we'd bought all the souvenirs we fancied, of course.

Margaretta and I had a special treat. We were flown from Calcutta to Darjeeling to do our recitals at a boys' public school up there. The two hours jeep ride from the nearest airport was spectacular, but jolting and very wet, so breaking our journey at a tea garden had a pleasant sound, conjuring up visions of comfort, elegance and cucumber sandwiches. What we got was a trip round a factory followed by lethally strong tea laced with Nestlé's Milk.

We'd been met at the airport by the headmaster, who I had growing suspicions was a bit of a prat. These were confirmed when we got to the school and found it was like a little Eton. Cricket was played of course, on a mud pitch, but any boy not engaged in recognised sporting activity had to freeze into immobility at the approach of a master clad in cap and gown. And not a white face to be seen but ours and the head's. All those Nepalese and Indian boys being brought up as perfect little English gentlemen. I daresay I was prejudiced against the headmaster by his muscling in on my performance. I'd just done my Ogden Nash bit (What was it doing in a programme about the English seasons? Chasing laughs as usual) when he interrupted with "Ah, my favourite poet!" and launched into a performance of his own.

The highlight of the trip for me was a visit to the Himalayan Institute where we were shown round by Tensing Norgay, an amazingly modest and obliging man. I left my gloves behind and he ran after me with them – this man who'd been up Everest twice! I looked on him with awe but the Head was chiefly impressed that "a chap like that" could send his sons to the school. Everest was lost in clouds so we never saw it, but Darjeeling was an atmospheric little place, rambling up the hills, cool and rainy, probably much as it was when the memsahibs of the British Raj took to the hills for the hot season. Certainly the heat in Calcutta seemed almost unbearable when we returned, but it was only a couple of days before we were off with the rest of the company to Hong Kong.

Amazing descent in the middle of the city, slipping neatly in between skyscrapers, wonderful food (but I'll never master chopsticks) tai chi in the park (just join in if you're passing, it seems to go on for ever) skimming over the water to Portuguese-built rococo Macau, strangely quiet and gently decaying, and to top all this – the Chinese Opera. The more determined culture vultures among us took the ferry to Kowloon after our show and made our way to the open-air theatre, where an enormous audience happily squeezed up to make room for us. I felt quite at home; it was very like the Working Men's Clubs, with not only drink but food served throughout, and cheerful but by no means exclusive attention being paid to the performance. This particular opera had started in the afternoon and was still in full swing when we left at 2 a.m. They say they sometimes last three days. There was plenty to look at but the music wasn't easy and of course we hadn't much idea what it was all about, so when we'd had an hour or so of it, tried a little of the food and exchanged grins and nods and handshakes with our neighbours, we decided to see if they'd let us backstage. The enormous communal dressingroom (no women in the cast of course) was like a huge bedsit. Actors asleep, eating, chatting, dressing and undressing and – of most interest to us – having their elaborate make-up applied. They accepted our presence without surprise, nodding amiably as they got on with things and hardly noticing when we left. It was now nearly four o'clock, with no sign of any transport and we were seriously con-templating sleeping in the street when a solitary cab appeared and was persuaded to let us sit on each others' laps, and miraculously there was a ferry. Of course we played it all up with the rest of the company, boasting that we'd had a unique cultural experience, but our rivals pulled rank by making the day trip to the New Territories and swanking about their experience of Red China, though, when pressed, they admitted they'd only seen a lot of paddy fields. I wonder I didn't join them because I've got this rather childish urge to collect countries, and China would have brought me to three dozen.

I've got 52 now, I think. It's confusing the way they keep shifting their borders and changing their names.

Singapore seemed almost ordinary after Hong Kong. It had this rather straitlaced regime which frowned on, among other things, long hair for men, so half our chaps' heads were a mass of kirbygrips under hastily acquired hats. The streets were clean, beggars were few and it was all very pleasant and rather tame. The best place to eat was the car park, which at night became a maze of stalls competing with their own special delicacies. You could go on from there to the intriguing and rather perplexing Boogis Street, the exclusive and almost, it seemed, official haunt of transvestites. Any time after midnight you could sip a beer in a clean, brightly lit outdoor café and watch "The Girls". It didn't seem like voyeurism because they obviously revelled in being watched. Occasionally someone would ask permission to photograph them and they would perch on a knee or accept a drink, but mostly they just wandered about between the tables looking coolly seductive. Maybe they were prostitutes but there was never much sign of a pickup; it looked as if they just wanted to parade as beautiful women. And lots of them were smashers, none more so than those who had turned the trick twice, got up to look like girls dressed as boys. It seemed strange that the nannyish régime didn't crack down on it. Perhaps the tourist board wouldn't let them; there were always lots of Americans at the tables.

We were getting used to exotica by Kuala Lumpur so even the exquisite railway station, more elaborate than many a temple, didn't excite us, and in fact what I chiefly remember about KL, was being taken out to dinner by a Chinese magnate whom I'd played tennis with in London, who took it for granted we needed a bodyguard to take us back to the hotel. I suppose some of the countries we visited were dangerous but none of us got attacked, or even stolen from in any great way. Things went missing from hotel rooms now and then but that can happen anywhere.

We went right up the Malay Peninsula with the exception of Brunei, which wouldn't let us in. Accommodation was a good deal rougher than anything to date; we came to take cockroaches for granted, and rats weren't unusual. At an official reception I drew the waiter's attention to the rats running under the chairs against the wall. "Issall right," he reassured me, "They just come for the food."

From somewhere in Borneo the US Navy took us on a three-hour trip upriver to the longhouse home of a Dyak tribe.

Headhunting was supposed to have been wiped out but there were some sly smiles if one mentioned it so we were agog as to what we might see. We were received by the head of the tribe in full ceremonial dress and led onto the long platform which joins the separate rooms making up a longhouse, the whole thing built on posts sunk upright in the water. The one we went to stretched maybe 100 yards, the communal part spread with beautifully patterned rush rugs. A large number of people had gathered to meet us and we were sat round in a circle, anxiously remembering, as we'd been told, not to point our feet into the middle. They then passed round their homemade hooch, and shortly after we were quite glad to have drunk it as the next thing to appear was a live cockerel with its comb sliced off so that the blood could be smeared on our cheeks in welcome. Warning looks from the American missionaries who were our minders told us we mustn't object, but when we were asked to indicate our leader so that he could have the honour of cutting off the cockerel's head, we all treacherously pointed at our director, an amiable young man but not what you'd call bloodthirsty. This time the missionaries intervened and explained it was against his religion so the cockerel disappeared and perhaps lived on. We now made our offerings of whiskey and Murraymints, which went down very well, and as we were all pretty lively by this time, including the missionaries, we happily let our hosts teach us their dance, which was mostly stamp and shuffle. Then we led them round in a conga and collapsed for more hooch and whiskey, not really caring by now where our feet were pointing. Some of us were then welcomed into their rooms, where the beautiful traditional artwork gave way to Coca-Cola signs and girlie calendars. Then at last we were invited to explore the whole longhouse, and there they were. Nothing too gruesome, not complete heads or anything, just human skulls. Six of them mounted on poles over the ashes of a fire. They were rather blackened but the most fascinating thing was that their mouths were filled with rice. Yes, our missionary guide said, it was a point of honour to keep them fed. "How old would they be?" I asked.

"Well of course they say they were put there before the practice was outlawed," she said, "But I was here three years ago and I only remember four then. Better not to ask. I think the practice is dying out gradually. A man used to have to present one to his bride's father but I think now it's mainly grudges being paid off." The Dyak man standing by. nodding and smiling, obviously thought we were being told all we needed to know.

Penang's a beautiful island and our hotel was separated from the bright blue sea only by date palms, but since we had two days off we decided to go and stay overnight in a resort up the coast. From there eight of us, having stocked up with chicken legs and gin, took a boat to an uninhabited island. We were so knocked out by the beauty of the place when we arrived – rich jungle, white sand, crystal clear water and no-on there but us – that we told the boat not to come back until noon the next day, planning to lie all night under the stars. We were the pick of the company, all kindred spirits, and the first thing we did was throw off all our clothes and rush about naked, in and out of the sea. When darkness fell, Gerry, our lighting man, who seldom spoke and had been immersed for most of the tour in "Zen and the Art of Motorcycle Maintenance", lit a fire and we started our barbecue. Then the storm started. Brilliant, continuous lightning and deafening thunder, with rain positively bouncing off the sand. In a few moments we'd been virtually hosed down. We were too scared to go into the jungle; even if the trees didn't come down, we'd seen monkeys there and who knew what else was lurking? Some of us took refuge in the sea, until we were fastened on by leeches. Where the hell had they come from, they hadn't been there in the daylight! The storm crashed on and showed no signs of abating, so finally we crouched together, hugging our knees in the sand. Then Donald Pickering, who'd staggered off in despair, shouted that he'd come across a shelter. It was tiny, just a corrugated iron roof, but we all managed to get under it by standing bolt upright. All that is except the miraculous Gerry, who produced a tarpaulin from somewhere and rigged up a shelter over the fire. He kept it going for the whole three freezing hours we spent under that roof, and when the rain finally stopped he'd actually got a billycan full of boiling water we could mix with our gin.

Eventually the sun came up in a cloudless sky so we could take off our soaking clothes and spread them to dry. Then we cooked the chicken and tore it to bits with some rather sodden bread and were into the water again, where the leeches had given place to some repellent but unthreatening sea slugs. So when the boat came to rescue us we were almost reluctant to leave. In fact I think Philip York and Jan Walters stayed behind. Was that the budding or the flowering of their romance, I wonder? Phil and I were good mates and I'd sometimes given him a lift to rehearsals in Watford. On one journey I said "Who do you think will be sleeping with whom by the end of the tour?" and he said "The one I really fancy is Jan." This seemed a bit uppity, as she was the leading lady and he was like me, one of the also-rans. They've been together now for – what? Twenty-five years? with two very good looking grown up kids. Phil and I played tennis whenever we could find a court and just once, in Kuala Lumpur, I beat him. When we're in company and I give him the nod he has to bring this up and embroider it a bit. Last time I "wiped the court with him!" In return I gave him my racquet when I reluctantly realised people were being kind playing with me. I wrapped it up like a bouquet and got it handed up to him at the end of a show at the Orange Tree. And he used it to win the mixed doubles at the Equity Tournament.

Don't point or eat with your left hand (that's the one you wipe your bottom with) don't rest your wrist on a car window (someone will cut your wristwatch off). Can that be all I remember of Jacarta? Seems like it.

Thailand though, our last country (40 for me), was something else again. "Watts and klongs," people who've been there tell you. "Don't miss the watts and klongs." Of course they could say temples and canals but we're all liable to that sort of travelupmanship. The temples are like wildly kitsch stage sets, fantastic architecturally, brilliantly painted and gilded, and all looking as if they were put up yesterday. The main one houses what's claimed to be the world's biggest buddha. It's certainly large, like a huge gold rolypoly baby, not very awe-inspiring. Anna's blackboard's on view too, the one she taught Yul Brynner's children with. If you go up the klongs in a punt you collect little boys fore and aft as a matter of course. As one drops off another takes his place. It seems to be not so much a joy ride as a recognised mode of transport between the wooden houses on the banks. Only half of the house is on land and most of life takes place on the apron over the water. They line the klongs all the way out from the city and a punt trip is a great way to see how a lot of urban Thais live.

We got a chance to see rural Thailand when we took a plane to Cheng Mai, the beautiful hill resort. From there we walked in the misty, rolling country, bought hand-crafted souvenirs in the villages, watched the elephants being brought down to bathe, and I, for one, forgot all about work. The only planes which could land in these parts were too small to take the "Pygmalion" set, and no-one wanted to hear my poetry so I was free as a bird to explore during the daytime and make friends at night with the marooned ex-pats, most of them fed up with all that beauty and dying for a gossip. By the end of the week I knew a lot about the rivalries, intrigues and love life of the Cheng Mai hill station.

It's strange how you can live intimately and happily with a group of people for months on end and then just as happily go your separate ways and never meet again. Two of that group are still my friends, and I once met the ever-resourceful Gerry on a job, but usually it's great fun and then it's over. I like it though. It's good meeting new people all the time, and if you're working together, unless someone's a real pain, you have a lot in common, and actors are great company anyway, after all they're programmed to entertain.

Chapter 15

Two of my happiest years were with the Royal Shakespeare Company. Well, on tour and at Stratford anyway; no-one likes working at the Barbican. Theatre architects! Will they never be persuaded to consult the people who are going to work in their precious edifices? The dressingrooms for the Pit are 76 stairs away from the stage. Yes, there are lifts, but you can't trust them, and you can find yourself clattering down stone staircases in high heels and trailing dresses, throwing yourself on stage at the last minute. The air conditioning seems designed expressly to give actors dry throats, and the greenroom is the dreariest of underground caverns. There's not a scrap of atmosphere or comfort anywhere backstage. And no pass door if you please. To get from front of house to backstage you have to go out into the street, as I found to my consternation during the run of "The Philistines". I had a twelve-minute wait in the third act so thought I'd shoot up in the little lift next to the stage, which didn't of course serve the dressingrooms, to Level Seven, which houses the Big Chiefs and also various office machinery. I wanted to duplicate some stuff for the Women's Group, which was just getting under way. Spying another little lift near to the machine and starting to panic about missing my entrance, I got in it and pressed the bottom button. It disgorged me, in Edwardian costume and wig, into the main concourse, and it was only by fighting my way through the crowds, up the stairs, into the street and in through the stagedoor that I got on the stage in time. The National's no better, people say. I can only speak for the miles of corridors you have to traipse if you want to see a friend after the show, but there's a story that Peggy Mount landed up in the wrong play. Nottingham's handsome theatre has such tiny dressingrooms that if you want to rest between shows you have to stretch out in the corridor, and when I was in the company that opened the Sheffield Crucible we found ourselves dressing in the offices, which far outnumbered the dressingrooms.

I seem to have got deflected. I was saying how happy I was with the RSC. I joined to play Rebecca Nurse in Arthur Miller's wonderful play "The Crucible". I was excited about the whole thing, so when games and exercises started at rehearsals I told myself firmly that this was how serious, established companies worked these days, and I must have faith in its lending subtlety and depth to my acting. For "The Crucible" we were each given a subject to research. Mine was witchcraft in 17th century England, as compared to its practice in America. I duly borrowed the appropriate books, mugged up the subject and wrote and submitted my piece. Nothing further was heard of it or of any of the papers turned in by the rest of the cast. Well, perhaps it helped our performances, who am I to say? Rehearsals went well anyway. I was very happy to be working with lots of really good people, and it was great getting to know and like each other in the pub at lunchtime. "The Winter's Tale", which we were rehearsing at the same time, also involved a certain amount of game-playing, but it was easier to see the point this time, since in Act IV we had to improvise a sort of Bohemian knees-up. We were rung up one night and told to bring a musical instrument next day and be prepared to play it. Some actual instruments appeared and were played after a fashion, a stick was rattled on a bicycle wheel, drums were bashed, combs and paper blown into, and I, chasing laughs as ever, flourished my Walkman. Some of the cast thought it was funny but the director wasn't amused.

Ours was what they called the Small Scale Tour, but in fact our sets were so elaborate and difficult to erect that to our ill-concealed delight we couldn't play on Mondays. We played swimming baths, sports halls, one marquee, one church and three cathedrals. I sat in Edward the Confessor's throne in Ely cathedral. Or I may have got the king and the cathedral mixed but I know it felt like being part of history. Many of the towns we visited had been starved of theatre so we got good houses everywhere. It was pretty painful finding town after town devastated by the decline in industry, but the welcome we got and the people we met made it all seem hearteningly worthwhile. We were lucky, too, to be playing sports halls, since all the facilities were thrown open to us. Half a dozen of us had brought our tennis racquets and before long we'd enthused practically the whole company, so we played every day it didn't rain and finished up with a hotly contested tournament. I had my 71st birthday on this tour and was given a great big party, with a tennis court cake, and our own musicians to accompany the rather rude words I'd put to "I'm 71 today." I was wearing wigs or headdresses in both plays so I'd got one of the wig mistresses to dye my hair bright pink with blue highlights. This wasn't common then, even for the young, so with my 70-year-old face it got some startled looks in the street but I felt I had to cock a snook at my advancing years. Later I had it dyed green for a party at Christopher Hampton's but when he opened the door he just said "What a pretty dress."

Companies often take their character from a leading member and we were lucky to have Alun Armstrong playing Leontes and John Proctor. I don't know that he did any leading particularly, except over the miners' strike, and he couldn't be induced to play tennis, but somehow he gave a solidity to the company, just by being not only a good actor but a straightforward, unpretentious, friendly chap; a mensch in fact. Thatcher's confrontation with the miners was on and while we were in Darlington he arranged for us to take the money we'd collected among us to a rally in a nearby mining village. A couple of carloads of us went and it was a moving experience, falling in behind the miners on the march through this sad little village they were desperate to save. "We Will

Win" it said on a square of cardboard held by a solitary woman on the kerbside. Arthur Scargill turned up at the rally and people went wild. Whether he got his strategy right or not in the event, there was no doubt of his support that day. Alun was still collecting when we got to Spitalfields at Christmas to play in an architecturally magnificent but freezing Hawksmoor church. This time he decided people might like to give money for toys for the miners' kids, and provided half a dozen yellow buckets for us to shake in people's faces as they left after he'd made his curtain call appeal. Practically everyone coughed up.

We were all wildly excited after this to get an invitation to take the plays to Poland. This was in 1984 and we'd be the first foreign company to visit the country after the repeal of martial law. Our sets needed large spaces, as we were playing in the round, or rather the long thin oblong, with audiences on all sides, so our first venue was a huge empty film studio in Warsaw. We shared the building with a bat, whose presence was admitted but not explained. Perhaps it was a mascot or left over from a horror film? It didn't appear a great deal, just enough to keep you in a state of terror. Warsaw was ankle-deep in snow and very beautiful in the old centre, lovingly reconstructed from old plans and Canaletto paintings. The film showing this devastation and the heroic voluntary work of restoration by the Warsaw citizens was staggeringly impressive and an unanswerable justification for what might have seemed a sentimental, even kitsch enterprise. Not that Poland was lacking in kitsch. The Christmas decorations were still in the churches; Mickey Mouse, toy trains, spacemen, anything to hand it seemed, all mixed up with angels, tinsel, Baby Jesuses and candles. We'd all brought goods in short supply - fruit, toothpaste, soap, chocolate, tea, instant coffee and a range of exotic toiletries. Lemons went down particularly well with the old ladies cleaning the churches, and once when I produced a slab of Cadbury's Fruit and Nut, all four women who were clearing the street dropped their snow shovels and fell upon it.

We did a Lord and Lady Bountiful act before the show too,

since our production had us wandering among the audience before the lights went down. Sometimes people looked a bit startled when a tube of toothpaste or a stick of deodorant was thrust at them but we hoped they got the idea. The shops were certainly bare and such goods as were on offer were depressingly shoddy. A row of almost identical dresses would be flanked by a few sad-looking shoes on one side and a pyramid of blocks of salt on the other. Perhaps understandably the assistants were lugubriously unforthcoming. The staff at our hotel were more actively hostile, seeming to keep us waiting deliberately and making no effort to understand our halting requests. You could understand their gall, as the food, while quite good, was well beyond the means of anyone but foreigners or the blackmarketeers who swarmed in the foyer. It wasn't easy to get past these touts, and the men among us had equal trouble with the prostitutes who wanted to take them up to the top floor. As usual the local actors were welcoming. They introduced us to the Artists' Club, which had a convivial atmosphere, especially as the evening wore on. If you ordered vodka the bottle appeared on the table and stayed there until it was exchanged for the next one. We managed some rowdy conversations despite the language difficulty, but my elementary Russian was greeted with stony glares. German was acceptable though.

I managed to get to three theatres, the best of which was a Youth Company musical. It was light, fast and impressively virtuosic but our Polish friends wrote it off as trivial and recommended the Ibsen playing upstairs. This was a three-hander unknown to me and the acting seemed pretty heavy-handed, particularly by the corseted, highly made-up leading lady. When I chatted to the director afterwards I couldn't bring myself to mention her and instead praised the two supporting men. He then gave me a lift home and introduced her as his wife. My final excursion was to the Jewish theatre. Was it in Hebrew or Yiddish? I can't remember. Anyway the simultaneous Polish translation didn't help and I crept out at the interval. I'd have stuck it if it had been good but it was pretty bad by any standards. The lad playing the SS soldier had hair down to his shoulders and compensated by strutting about in a continuous goose-step.

Usually I found myself alone on the culture trail, but the company went en masse to the church of the young priest who'd famously been murdered by the police. The railings were hung with defiant banners and the slow-moving four-deep queue went nearly round the churchyard. We were made to go to the head of it, which thankfully no-one seemed to resent. It was some time since the assassination but the churchyard was still full of massed flowers and tributes, leading to a car like the one in which he'd been abducted. The open boot was ringed by fairy lights and inside was a plastic Baby Jesus. This may have seemed kitsch to Western eyes but it was obviously in tune with the dignified mourning and defiance of the people in the queue.

Meanwhile we were getting great houses and receptions for the plays, particularly "The Crucible" with its message of desperate dissent. A school group was supposed to be coming from Gdansk to our matinee but the trip was cancelled at the last moment so a handful of the pupils came on their own, overnight by train. Another actor and I agreed to talk to them between shows and they proved to be a sophisticated, knowledgeable lot. I issued a blanket invitation to anyone who could get an exit visa and a year later one of the boys managed it, after a lot of hanging about at embassies, his end and mine. He arrived with several tins of ham which he used for his daily sandwiches, and a beautiful embroidered tablecloth which I can't bring myself to use. Most of his time was spent in Tottenham Court Road acquiring more and more sound equipment, and he finally staggered off to the airport practically invisible under a mass of cartons. I guess we'd all been a bit rash with our invitations, thinking no-one could get out of Poland, so we were caught on the hop in Stratford when a whole band phoned from Birmingham asking for beds for the night. We sorted out mattresses and sleeping bags and so on, and then waited for them to arrive, which they did, in hilarious spirits, at 3 a.m.

They probably came from Lwow, our second venue, which was more friendly than the capital but without, superficially at least, much to offer in the way of excitement. We went back to Warsaw airport by coach at night and a terribly gloomy journey it was. Snowy wastes interspersed with sad little villages or towns, dimly lit and deserted. At the airport though some of our audiences. from both towns were waiting with flowers and gifts, so we left in an atmosphere of great warmth and emotion, which took us all the way home on the plane, helped by unexpectedly free vodka.

While in Warsaw I'd been asked by Barry Kyle if I'd like to come to Stratford to play a rough old prostitute who took bets on how far she could run while peeing. It seemed a likely part so I agreed, provided some other equally challenging roles could be found. Eventually I played the tight-minded mother in Gorki's "The Philistines" and the Countess in "Les Liaisons Dangereuses", both in the Other Place, four minutes from my flat over the river and right next to the local tennis club where the company had twenty free memberships. How much better could life get? To walk through Shakespeare's own churchyard, though not alas to

"The Philistines' with Griff Jones

'The Philistines', Royal Shakespeare Co. at Stratford-on-Avon. 1984

With Penny Ryder in "The Dillon".

act in one of his plays, and to go to sleep to the sound of rushing water. Only two snags, the river was too polluted to swim in and they charged to visit the actual grave, so I had to forgo my hoped-for daily dip and homage. Still, the plays were fun. "The Dillon" had been done the year before and surprisingly its revival was equally successful. Based on a local author's account of an artisan's life in the town at the turn of the century, it followed him through the first World War and to his end in the workhouse. It was a lot livelier than that sounds, with Peggie Mount a tower of strength as Dillon's mother, one of the actors chucked in the river nightly, a brass band, a horse and cart, and me making determined efforts to get a stream of pee going. Last year's actress had settled for mime but I was determined to have a go. Sadly the lemonade bottle with tube issuing through a hole I'd embroidered in my knickers never produced more than a measly dribble and eventually I was forced to accept failure when Ron Cook, possibly feeling his oats in his first eponymous role, shouted to me to get out of the way so he could get on with the next scene.

The play started in the Other Place and then took to the streets, parks and open ground around the town. The audience came along, accompanied by a couple of dozen local people, all in costume, who joined in the action as required. At the interval there were camp fires and hot food before the big War scene, then everyone was given a flare, and the band led us solemnly past the war memorial as Paul Webster read out the names of the dead. I cried every night at this point though I was supposed to be singing. It was tremendously imaginative and affecting, and although we had pretty awful weather none of the audience chickened out. At least, they were all there in the theatre for the last scene, though it's possible a few fainthearts peeled off and lurked there on some of the wetter nights.

Each year at Stratford there was a sort of in-house festival. The actors were given the chance to put on their own shows for a matinée performance at the Other Place, the smallest of the three theatres. We could do anything we fancied – solo acts, musicals, plays, revues, all with the backing of the RSC's resources. I'd got a play that needed an airing. It had gone down well at a rehearsed reading at the Orange Tree a couple of years before and it was on a subject I felt strongly about, so – let's stir a bit of politics into the mixture. It featured an unreconstructed old communist grannie (Guessoo) who goes to Greenham Common, kicks a policeman and gets put in gaol. And for good measure there's a black boy on probation who pals up with her and a grandson-in-law who's in nuclear research. And of course it's a comedy. I was very lucky in my cast, generously giving their time, working enthusiastically and turning in performances I could only have dreamed of. They were Francine Morgan, Keith Odhams, Geraldine Wright, William Haden, Paul Webster, and me. We didn't have a black boy in the company so I was allowed to hire a lad, and he was fine – brought in quite a few people too – but as we didn't have a programme I can't give his name. Alan Rickman did a splendid poster of me behind bars and the performance was a great credit to everyone, getting all its laughs and. hopefully making some of its points. When I'd had the idea for the play I hadn't been to Greenham Common, though I'd followed the activities there with admiration. (I don't have to explain, do I, that Greenham Common was a U.S. base that was picketed night and day for years and years by a large number of heroic women who camped round it and made constant efforts to disrupt its activities?) Although the play didn't actually go there I realised I needed to know more about it, so I borrowed a sleeping bag and some kind friends drove me down. The group on Blue Gate, the first one I came to, greeted me warmly and weren't at all snooty about my only staying one night. Later, half of us went off to a pub, leaving the other half on duty. This seemed to be the usual pattern and though it felt like skiving since I'd just arrived I told myself it was the best way to get to know them. Shortly after we came back, a convoy did come out and we did a bit of harassing and attempting to delay them, then it was settling down for the night, first round a little fire, then in makeshift tents. It was a long night and very cold so that when, waking from half-sleep, I heard birdsong, I thought – at last, the dawn chorus! It was blooming nightingales. My admiration for those women was enormously increased by just that one chilly night. Lots of them were there for years. And so cheerful and friendly. The neighbours weren't though, I got shouted at a bit as I made my way to the station.

As the season neared its end Terry Hands, the boss, called all the women in the company to a meeting and informed us that we were such an outstanding talented and dynamic group he was prepared to give us a theatre at the Barbican with all the backing we needed to put on our own production. This flummoxed the hell out of us. We didn't quite believe we were so special and wondered if there was some sort of hidden agenda, but we couldn't refuse of course so we spent all our spare time hammering out our proposals. Women's issues? Men in the cast? Female author? Female director? Big or little theatre? Parts for all of us? By the time we moved to the Barbican we were still in the discussion stage, but then Juliet Stevenson introduced us to Sue Todd, a director of great enthusiasm, drive and personal conviction. Under her sway we embarked on an intensive course of improvisation and research, after which Sue introduced Debora Levy, a poet and playwright, who engaged to shape our improvisation into a play. This was a perfectly good idea but unfortunately for me I didn't admire Debora's work (she brought along a group of actors to do a short play of hers) and I increasingly felt Sue had taken over the group and was running it to suit herself. I wrote to her saying this and bowing out but to my surprise she rang me up and asked me to reconsider. Some of the others also asked me not to desert what they felt was an increasingly leaky ship, and I did try, but it was hopeless and as I had no other part at that time I resigned from the company. The play eventually went on, with stars brought in to take over some of the parts enthusiastically created by the original women. It got torn to pieces by the critics but one of the girls who stayed with it claimed it developed a cult following. Anyway that was the end of my stint with the RSC. I could have gone to the West End with "Liaisons" but after the relaxed schedule of repertoire I jibbed at a long run of eight performances a week and decided I'd go back to telly or anything else that turned up. Maybe something in the Fringe?

I hadn't done much Fringe but what I had done I'd enjoyed. This had been mainly at the Orange Tree Theatre in Richmond, then a room over a pub, now also an elegant theatre in the next road, still run by the indomitable Sam Walters, who I often think they could do with at the National. My only reservation is his penchant for keeping the cast hanging about in the acting area between scenes, trying to make themselves inconspicuous. The first play I did there I was provided with a curtain and a chair but I still had to listen to the play night after night. In the next production it was even worse. We had to crouch behind the seats, trying not to catch the eyes of punters peering round at us. As an audience, I loathe the gimmick, largely discontinued thank heaven, of having the actors bounce about in the auditorium, making the audience "part of the show", and this was still worse. After a couple of nights I allowed a jolly little dance to take me through the door to backstage, and I was peacefully stretched out on the broken-down sofa when Sam walked through. "Are you ill?" he asked in alarm. "No, no, just tired." "But how will you get back?" "Don't worry; I've worked it out." So with a dubious look he went on his way. I had something like the same encounter with Peter Hall in his production of "Orpheus Descending." Finding that I was required to spend a whole scene peering, with half a dozen others, through a window, "Peter," I said. "I don't want to do this living frieze stuff, it makes me feel a failure." "But how will you get off?" "Well I won't go on" I said, and he acquiesced. You can take co-operation and commitment just so far.

Anyway Sam continued to ask me to work for him and it was in a very successful musical of "The Little Match Girl" that I went stone deaf. I woke up with the phone ringing and a guest shaking me awake and with no hearing at all. It didn't come back for over a week, during which I was most unusually doing two jobs, a telly by day and the show at night. It was funny scurrying about between jobs in total silence; I drove quite a few miles on the motorway in second gear. They shot all my stuff in close-up, which worked all right, but at night I was in trouble, not only with picking up cues but not knowing what key I'd pitched on. I gave up on the chorus numbers after catching the pianist's eye, but when it came to my own songs I just launched into them and trusted him to adapt as required. Then Sam asked me to direct a lunchtime two-hander, but the woman's part was such a gift I couldn't bear not to play it so I didn't establish myself as a Fringe director.

The only other Fringe venues I've worked at are the King's Head in Islington, where you could only whisper in the tiny unisex dressingroom and couldn't flush the lavatory during the show, and the Almeida, also in Islington, but perhaps too posh to be called Fringe and, because it was run by a couple of actors when I was there, a very pleasant place to work. The girl in the box office gave a party and served the most scrumptious sweet I've ever tasted. Here's the recipe:-

Almond Base with Sherry Cream

6 egg whites.
300gr icing sugar.
300gr ground almonds.

Whisk the egg whites until stiff.
Mix the almonds and sugar together then carefully fold into the egg whites.
Bake at 165o for about 45 minutes, until firm and golden brown. (It is advisable to line the cake tin with greaseproof paper.)

6 egg yolks.
6 dessertspoons caster sugar.
1 cup sherry.

Mix and heat gently over a low heat, stirring all the time, until thick as custard. Cool to below body temperature.

Whip 300-400 mls cream and mix with the chilled custard mixture. Spread over the almond base and serve.

We needed a few treats as we were doing a modern writer's version of "Hippolytus" with a Romanian director and it was all those games again! I thought we'd never get down to rehearsal. Janet Suzman, who was playing Phaedra, brought a very elegant screen into the dressingroom and put it round her place. I was tempted to hang a star on it but as we were going to be together for a while I restrained myself. I was playing one half of a Chorus, an old peasant with a stick, and for a lot of the play was perched on top of a high wall. Staggering about up there I crashed into the corner of a rostrum and hacked a lump out of my leg. Fortunately it didn't matter if I stayed sitting until the end of the play, but with mistaken kindness the management put me in a cab to the local hospital, where I hung about far into the night and then couldn't find a taxi in the deserted City streets.

I'm given to bashing my legs, always, come to think of it, the same one. I'd crashed into a table I had to move on the RSC tour and had to have stitches, then I'd done myself a really alarming injury at home, tripping on the telephone flex and falling onto a spike at 4.30 when I was playing at Stevenage that night. I got myself to hospital, where of course they said "Please take a seat," then I rang the theatre to say I might not make it, and after a very long hour while a very young doctor dithered as to whether to stitch it or tape it, I managed to get a taxi, ring my agent from Victoria to tell the theatre to meet the train, and fling myself onto it among all the commuters, mildly curious about this dishevelled old girl with one leg of her trousers blood soaked from knee to ankle. The next six weeks of the tour were tedious as each new hospital poured scorn on the last one's treatment and did something entirely different. In Wales I was put in plaster and did a lot of the show sitting down, in Cambridge they used a special ointment and forbade me to touch the dressing for a week, though I did when it started to smell, then another hospital put me on crutches, until finally a doctor said I was suffering from multiple management and I should just let the air get to it. So I sat in my landlady's garden with my leg up, nervously batting away the flies, and it did the trick. I suppose it was vanity that made me so doggedly determined not to miss a show. I'd never been off in my life, and anyway I loved the part and didn't want anyone else getting my laughs.

Chapter 16

You couldn't say I've had a particularly distinguished film career. Bert started me off with a couple of parts in "Interpol", the series he was working on. You'd think I'd remember them – my first film parts – but I've no idea now what they were. Wives or mothers I daresay, Then after a while I got a corner in hatchet-faced housekeepers and the like, one, to my delight, with Rod Steiger. That was a very odd piece. He played an early suicide bomber, an Irish patriot trying to get into the opening of Parliament to blow up the Queen. I must have seen the film somewhere because I remember a lot of intercutting with newsreels, but I'm not sure it ever made it to a real cinema, and what Steiger was doing in it is a mystery. After he and I had privately agreed that the dialogue in our scenes was unplayable we made up our own. So – improvising with a Method actor from Hollywood and with my own caravan to boot – it felt like stardom.

I was grim-faced again as a highly starched hospital matron making life hell for Malcolm McDowell and Nanette Newman as a couple of paraplegics in "The Raging Moon". Michael Flanders was also in the cast and I did something which I still blush to remember. While I was talking to him in his wheelchair I put my hand kindly on his shoulder, not as the bossy matron but as me. He didn't shrug me off and I daresay he was used to it, but I still go hot at the thought of it. The screenplay was by Shelagh Delaney and I began to think I was a Delaney actress, since I'd done her second play "The Lion in Love" at the Royal Court and opened my second Bangor season with "A Taste of Honey". Bangor hadn't quite known what to make of that play. "Right enough" they said, "We know that sort of thing goes on over the water, but you'll not find it here." Shelagh also wrote the script for "Charlie Bubbles" in which I was Albert Finney's po-faced housekeeper. This was a fun job as well as being a lovable little film, and it actually had Liza Minelli in it, and not even in the lead! Albert was great to work with as a director and actor and we filmed in a house just down the road from me, so even when I wasn't called I could pop down there for lunch. This was the first time I'd had a stand-in and I was embarrassed to find she expected to fetch me tea and coffee and generally wait on me. I hated it and was worried about whether to tip her. I've never cracked the tipping problem and I suspect a lot of people haven't. I remember Maurice Denham saying "The make-up girls are sweet, aren't they? Do you tip them?" "Well no," I said, "Aren't we all just members of a team, doing our jobs?" "Yes," he agreed, "And they probably earn more than us anyway." But really, if we haven't got it sorted out by this time! A Dutchman told me a joke once. Three Englishmen are waiting to be hanged. "Come on, what's the hold-up?" says the hangman. "We were wondering how much to tip." Of course, come to think of it, people used to tip the headsman in the hope of a nice clean job.

I got quite a lot of respect from young people when they knew I was in "Pink Floyd – the Wall" even though I couldn't claim to have met Bob Geldof. As the headmaster's dragon of a wife who forced him to eat his gristle I was only in one scene and I'm not sure if I even said anything, but as the director was Alan Parker it was a prestige sort of job. I'd made a couple of commercials for Alan and rated him highly as a director and a person, so when my agent said "The casting director says Alan wants to find something for Marge", I was thrilled, though I couldn't pretend to understand the script. I never saw the film but I believe it achieved cult status.

One of the commercials I made for Alan got me a whole week

in Paris doing stills for it. I'd blown out my face in a scornful pout in Alan's film, so the French director's main cry was "Margery, blow, blow!" I must have got that right because he asked me to do an additional commercial, with French dialogue. I quite fancied my French but my fellow actress burst out laughing every time I said a word, and in the end I think they dubbed it. Nice job, though. Caviar and champagne for lunch and the make-up artists give you a facial as part of the service.

Another of my cult films was "The Princess Bride". I went to see the Hollywood director Rob Reiner at a little office up a lot of stairs, and was handed a script and told to look at the part of "The Ancient Booer". They put a chair out on the landing and suggested I sit out there and study it. There were about eight lines, leading up to a lot of booing and improvised invective, so I wasn't sure how much in-depth study I was supposed to do on the landing. However when I went back I yelled and snarled and booed with such abandon that he gave me the part on the spot, unusual with Americans, who are more likely to recall you three

'The Ancient Booer' - The Princess Bride

times for as many lines, after which you hear nothing until your agent tells you they've cast the part in the States. Rob Reiner may have regretted his rashness when we came to do the scene, as I got a nervous block and kept screwing up on one word. We were in the courtyard of a huge castle, with maybe a couple of hundred extras whom I had to address before screaming my abuse at the Princess. "You're filth, you're slime, you're refuse!" I was supposed to scream.

Now there's a story in my family about an old aunt inveighing against beggars. "Give them a broom and let them sweep up the refuge," she'd say. So of course that's what I said, time after time. I could feel it coming and I couldn't stop myself. "You're filth, you're slime, you're refuge!" again and again. *"Refuse!"* Reiner said with increasing emphasis. "Refuse, refuse" whispered the crowd at my elbow. "I know," I said desperately, "It's just – you see - I had this aunt – " I saw Reiner's eyes glaze over, arid hastily reassured him "It's all right, I know what it is. I'll get it right this time, I promise!" I did, finally, and carried on triumphantly to the end of the scene, after which the entire 200 extras cheered. Reiner came up to me in the restaurant that night and said the scene was great, without even mentioning the fatal word. It's only fair that films pay better than anything else because they take more out of you. Maybe if I did more I'd relax into it. It's true I took my part in "Howard's End" in my stride, but then most of it was cut and I featured mostly as a big hat in the distance, and a bit of impro in a car, with bossy old Emma Thompson telling her mum and me how to do it. Yes, I know, a terrific actor, splendid in "Love, Actually" and lots of other things, and then there's her screenplay for "Sense and Sensibility", far and away the best of the Jane Austen movies. Still, her mother, Phillida Law, is also a smashing actor and doesn't need any help.

I guess I'll never qualify as a pukka film actor. I've only just finally sorted out what a "best boy" does and I still don't know what a "dirty single" is. Of course I've done a lot of telly films but I'm not sure if they count. One which promised to be fun was set in the Brecon Beacons in Wales. This was by Julia Jones, an old friend from Amersham and Bangor, when she and her husband Benny had been in my first season there. Then Benny got desperately ill and Julie took up writing to keep them and their kids afloat. She turned out to be very good at it and this was the third play of hers I'd done. I was a repressed housewife on holiday, who had to wriggle out of her girdle and throw it to the winds, climb the hills, splash about in the river, defy her husband and generally "discover" herself. For the first of our scheduled three weeks we sat glumly in the minivan while the rain tippled down. Then a watery sun came out and we rushed down to the river. In the second shot I slid on the wet rocks and broke my leg, the usual one. So it was off to hospital where although it was only the ankle they put me in plaster up to my hip. The part could have been recast but they decided to get a double for the long shots, and for the next fortnight I was strapped on a stretcher and carried up and down precipitous gorges by a mountain rescue team, "Steady, bit dodgy this bit, think it's safe?" and then propped up behind bracken or rocks to get on with the acting. I'd worked with the double some time in the past and she didn't endear herself to me by putting on a curious waddle and saying she remembered that was how I walked. Still, it was a fun job. Nice director, James McTaggart, who kept his cool through all the adversities and only lost it when he wanted some service from the hotel staff and they were all glued to rugby on the box. Didn't he know we were in Wales?

My agent had told me a film script was on its way so I was cursing my luck until it arrived and the character turned out to be bedridden. The only snag was the opening shot, which read "Close-up of the hanging flesh of Mum, stretched naked on the bed." However when I went, still in plaster, to see the director he said he'd settle for just stripping to the waist. "You see," he explained earnestly, "I've got several nude sex scenes, and if I have a very much older woman also nude, then I won't be suspected of pornography." H'm. I hadn't in fact thought I'd mind stripping off, but I found it made me feel rather silly, especially after the make-up man had handed the sponge over to me when he got to the nipples. This was before we all went topless on the beaches and in fact I tabled a motion for the next Equity AGM requiring any director who wanted nudity to strip off himself. It didn't get passed but I believe more famous actresses have taken up the issue since. "Made" was the less than compelling title of the film, which wasn't at all bad, though it rather fell between stools in trying to combine a "slice of life" with a bid for the young audience by including a rock singer of ephemeral fame and no great charm. Our schedule went to pot when he was never to be found at the same address two mornings running. It was a cinema film but I doubt if it was widely shown, though it did mysteriously surface in Gozo when I was holidaying there. A dismayingly large number of Gozetans leered at me and asked if I'd minded taking my clothes off.

I've also sat on a bench in Hyde Park for two days while someone repeatedly hurled himself over my head into a lake, in "101 Dalmatians", and I had rather more to do as a nun-cum-nurse in a non-musical "Les Miserables", with Liam Nelson and Liv Ulman. She mystified me by providing her own make-up assistant to spray her between takes. Perhaps it makes you gleam? What else? Oh yes – "Love, Actually". Eight words, one of them "Oh". But Richard Curtis is a really nice man, I'd do eight words for him any day. After I'd agreed to do it I went to America on holiday and came back to find my agent on the phone saying they'd decided my character should be black. (They'd got a lot of flak for having so few blacks in "Notting Hill".) My offer to black up was turned down but later they decided they'd have me after all. We did it in a Wandsworth street and Hugh Grant was easy to work with and pleasant to the attendant crowd of fans. There was a huge wrap party, and I took my grandniece Emma, who was agog to meet all the stars, not one of whom turned up of course. I'd done myself up to the nines in my best Chinese satin coat and lots of baubles, and looked a right fool among all the jeans-clad technicians and their mates. Richard may have guessed how silly I felt because he came and talked to Emma and me for ages. As I say, a very nice man. Oh, and I had ten words in the latest "Harry Potter". Had I arrived at last?

Chapter 17

Some time in 1993 a script turned up for the second episode of a proposed series called "Peak Practice". Seeing that it was written by Lucy Gannon, a writer I admired, I eagerly searched for my character's scenes and found she had just one line. "I'm not doing that!" I said to my agent. "I think there's more in the next episode," she said. Nine years later I was still doing it, the only character to have gone right through the series. So I'd fallen on my feet late in life you might say. It was in fact a very, very nice job. Not only good scripts – Lucy Gannon didn't stay with us long after the first series, as the best writers seldom do, but the standard stayed high, with good believable characters and plots and plenty of gentle humour as well as some spectacular stuff. A good cast too, headed by Kevin Whately, Amanda Burton, Sylvia Sims, Simon Shepherd, Esther Coles and darling Maurice Denham, with whom I had a double act as a retired RAF pilot and his housekeeper. Maurice submitted a storyline for us to get married and develop Alzheimer's together but they wouldn't buy it.

On top of all this it was set in Derbyshire, one of the most beautiful counties in England. It was real bliss to be driven to all those different locations, through wonderful woods and hills and stone-built villages, even in winter, when it got very cold indeed. We used the same little town, with its church and shops around a square for our local village, dressing up the shops with new names and merchandise. The locals soon got to know our schedules, so there they'd be when we arrived, lining the square and cheerily greeting us. People seemed quite ready to let out their homes too, retiring upstairs while we crashed about on the ground floor. Some of them may have regretted it, especially the one with a gardenful of roses, when we cut off every single one because it was the wrong season.

The 'doctors' settled in little houses in the district, but the rest of us, who weren't in every episode, commuted and were put up in local hotels, mainly the Matlock Bath, which had a huge outdoor swimming pool surrounded by beautiful scenery and fed by water that came underground from Matlock Spa. Very healthy – and freezing! Always the same temperature though, so you could walk through snow and swim in it. As I did, of course, always the show-off. The trick was to fill your bath with scalding water, wrap up in towels and stagger through the snow, swim your ten lengths and get back just as the bathwater had cooled to the right temperature. And then boast about it to anyone who would listen. The ever – and over – solicitous Health and Safety people put the kybosh on my Derbyshire swimming by insisting on a lifeguard for the pool, which was promptly fenced in and closed except for the hours when I was working. These same busybodies had turned up with their clipboards at Swiss Cottage and changed the direction of swimmers in the lanes, so that you were swimming alongside people in the next lane instead of passing by them. When I asked why, they said it had been introduced in another pool and they thought it was something to do with the flow of the water! The tiny indoor pool in the Matlock Bath was a sad comedown but you could meet some interesting people in the sauna; I was often wedged in with three retired miners who were far from nostalgic about their working life and wouldn't have any of that nonsense about communities and camaraderie. It was a vile life, one of them said, only one degree better than seafaring. They weren't staying at the hotel of course; there was a club associated with the pool and lots of local people used it. Over the years I got to know the hotel staff quite well so it was a nice homely billet for me. I didn't think much of their food though, but as our caterers did a good line in starters I'd stock up at lunchtime and eat them in the evening in front of the telly, with a glass or so of my favourite tipple, rum and coke. Not a bad life.

My character, Alice North, a kind-hearted if contentious old village woman, was given quite a few storylines of her own as the series developed. I was mugged and burgled, I got stranded in the middle of the night on a boat, I had an abortive romance, I got stuck in the bath, I got put in a cell for not paying my poll tax, I gave bone marrow (at the age of 85) to my granddaughter, and of course I had every malady and accident under the sun so that I could turn up at the practice. I once suddenly appeared on a zimmer frame, having apparently had a hip replacement without a single week's wait; and I had my gall bladder out twice, but at decent intervals, so no-one seemed to notice. And then there were the chickens; I had rather too many sessions with them for my taste. I'm not exactly afraid of chickens but they do that rather alarming thrashing about when you pick them up, and in one episode I had to faint in their coop and spend then night with them. Of course not really a whole night but I was lying down with them at their level rather a long time and one of them tried to roost on me.

Now and then I got asked to go to functions targeted at old people, as a sort of role model, to show that life doesn't end at 80. I'd recite Jenny Joseph's defiant poem, "When I'm an old woman I shall wear purple," and dish the dirt on PP, and often I'd make a point of saying I wore hearing aids because I've got this campaign to make people less sensitive about wearing them. During our first read-through Maurice and I had inadvertently put our heads together and caused a piercing whistle, so we took to doing it as a trick.

I was lucky enough to intersperse other jobs with "Peaks", as we called it, and I was once in the studio in the daytime and Nottingham Playhouse at night, playing Mrs. Higgins in "Pygmalion", being whisked to and fro by car, feeling nice and important. I did "Reckless" too, a five-part TV play written by the wonderful Paul Abbott, whose work makes such a great case for drama against all those deadly reality shows. Robson Green was a nice chap to work with, though he stood me up on a date to swim in Lake Windermere before the day's work.

In the seventh year of "Peaks" someone up there decided it needed turning around to make it more appealing to the young, so the plots got a bit wild, with more sex and rather unlikely adventures. An evil bisexual nurse turned up and caused havoc all round, finally abducting the woman doctor on her wedding day and hurling them both off a cliff. "Hold on them as they hurtle to their fate," said the script. "To be continued." But it wasn't. Which was sad for me as I'd rather counted on it seeing me out, and instead I had to look for other work.

It was nearly a year before I found any, and then it was with one of my infrequent sorties into the West End, playing Anfiza, one of Chekhov's old nannies, in "Three Sisters" at the Playhouse. I love Chekhov next only to Shakespeare so it was sad that I didn't enjoy the job as much as I'd hoped. Maybe it was the stairs – 36 of them

'Three Sisters' at the Playhouse. Me poking my head among the stars

between the stage and the dressingrooms, so by the end of the run I'd climbed 21,000 of them in heavy costumes with underskirts and a bumbag – or maybe the part's too episodic or small, but I never really felt part of the play. My fault. The company was friendly and fun, the men especially. And I dressed with two very nice girls. Still, when some of the cast was changed after ten weeks I tried to get out. I suppose I just don't enjoy spending my evenings sitting in the dressingroom listening to the same play on the tannoy. Anyway, there were only six more weeks left of the run, so I settled down, trying to think I was lucky to be working. And of course it wasn't all boredom. The dressingrooms open onto a long if comfortless passage where you could brew coffee and socialise, and Robert Bathurst devised a fun quiz between the matinée and evening shows on Saturday. The men's dressingroom always won because Tom Beard's too knowledgeable by half.

There was an earlier West End run when I'd also been crossing off the days, this time at the Haymarket. Peter Hall's own company put on Tennessee Williams's "Orpheus Descending"

'Reckless' with Robson Green and Francesca Annis

with Peter directing. Again I struck lucky with my roommate. I wasn't sure I was going to like Amanda Walker when we met. A bit too elegant and socially poised, and I suspected she might be a Tory. We were playing sisters, funny old girls in cloche hats, a bit of a comedy act, so it was important to get on. We were polite and co-operative for the first few days, then one lunchtime she said shall we find a café and I said I'd rather find a pub, and we were friends. They were on-off-on-off parts but in our two longer waits we'd climb to our room and treat ourselves to a small but heartening tot of Scotch. Then we'd cross off another day on the calendar. A further little diversion was to visit Paul Freeman, marooned in bed on a high platform only visible when lit. We had a little scene with him so we'd get up there early, give him a little tot, and he'd recite, sotto voce, the Shakespeare sonnet I'd set him the previous day. Sounds precious but you've got to amuse yourself somehow. We did take our parts seriously though, Mandy and I, and seem to have done them rather well, as we got a disproportionate amount of space in the reviews.

The leading man's part was taken by a very beautiful young French Canadian called Jean-Marc Barr who'd just made a big hit in a film about deep sea diving, and the leading ladies were Vanessa Redgrave and Julie Covington. Vanessa knows what she wants to do and does it and Julie can most kindly be described as volatile, so poor Jean-Marc must have wished himself safely back under the water as the battles raged over his head. I met him in the street in Cardiff, where we opened, and I remember his piteous "Is theatre always like this?" I said I didn't know a lot about theatre at this level but I thought he might have struck unlucky. The play was set in the deep South and we all duly worked on our Southern drawl, but then Vanessa suddenly changed to an Italian accent. I daresay she cleared it with Peter but none of us lesser lights was warned, and as her character, though Italian-born, had come to the States at the age of two it didn't seem too plausible. But there you go – a star's a star. From Cardiff we went to Bath, where I heard Peter say something that really shocked me. We were still in trouble with one of our sets, and he said we shouldn't worry because we'd got a week before we opened. Doesn't anything matter but London and the critics? Mandy Walker and I remain friends and see each other now and then, always with pleasure, and when I was at the Almeida and she was away she gave me her keys so I could luxuriate in her comfortable house between shows. She had a most impressive, not to say formidable, mother; no longer a working actress but still very much a grande dame.

Chapter 18

From time to time when I was cooling my heels I'd try to make myself useful with good works, first with NACRO, which befriends ex-prisoners, in association with the probation service. I had moderate success with one or two clients – fixing accommodation, having them round for meals and so on – and I did duty at the sad little club in Camden Town which seemed just a refuge for hopeless recidivists, but I didn't have the right set-up for the work. You need a family home to welcome people into and give them a taste of a better life. One of my clients was a window-cleaner who said he wasn't sure but he thought my place was one of those he'd done over and as I've been burgled six times I was inclined to believe him. And then the next lad stole from me, which means you lose the client as well as the money and are considered a bit of a failure.

I had one success though and I still get a glow from it. My unlikely client was a girl of fourteen. Pat hadn't been to prison of course but she'd got mixed up with some kids who were breaking open electricity meters. I got to know her family quite well – they were Kilburn Irish – an elder sister, very bright, who turned down the chance of university because she felt out of place, two brothers, the younger of whom I unsuccessfully tried to teach to read, stupidly using a middleclass primer instead of comics, a labourer father and a very sweet but schizophrenic mother. Money was tight and the home was chaotic but it was the poor mother's condition which was the most trouble.

My siblings were all living in Kent now – we seem to be a clannish family – so I thought it might help if I gave the kids a look at the country, and started by taking Pat for a weekend at Grace's pub. That was when she saw her first live sheep. "Oh, aren't they lovely! Can you pat them?" Then I took her and the boys for a week at Westgate-on-Sea where Kate had a flat to let. That was a mixed success. Pat was deep into a book and couldn't be budged from the house, but Bert took over the boys and gave them a good time musselling and so on, though they weren't very keen on actual swimming. Unfortunately, my car broke down on the way back and caused a long wait. Pat was sympathetic but the boys got bored and morose and finally we parted without a word.

Meanwhile their poor mother had been put in Colney Hatch Hospital. She was allowed out with supervision so I could take her, and sometimes Pat and the boys, for trips to Hampstead Heath or wherever. Then they transferred her to a ward with violent patients and she begged me to get her out. I bearded a doctor, who was most sympathetic and promised faithfully to get her moved. Next week when I went, that doctor had gone back to India and she was back in the violent ward, if she'd ever been out of it. She'd got used to it by now and made friends with some of the quieter patients, and she said I mustn't worry, but I knew I'd let her down. So why did I say that this was my one success? Because Pat did so well. She not only ditched her dodgy friends and got on with her education but then, to my awestruck delight, she landed a job as P.A. to a woman MP. Then she went on to marry, move to Ireland, have children and grandchildren while simultaneously acquiring more qualifications, and now, in her 50th year, she's doing her final two terms at Swansea University. And she wrote to me at Christmas saying I was the one who'd made her see it was all possible.

My only other attempt at good works, apart from serving in charity shops, where you can buy the pick of the goods dirt cheap, which is nice if hardly the idea, was with adult literacy. My favourite pupil was an elderly (well, probably younger than me) West Indian lady. Unfortunately she was stuck on the Bible, and the Old Testament at that, but I weaned her on to Bible Tales for the Young and she made very good progress, at writing too. I managed to keep myself to myself as the unlikely tales unfolded but when we got to the Immaculate Conception she challenged me direct. "Do you believe it?" "Well I've never heard of it actually …" "But God can move mountains." "Erm …" "And everyone in the whole world believes it." "Well I don't know about –" "Well everyone in Cricklewood believes it." The clincher. I wasn't about to argue, I just accepted the coffee heavily laced with rum which routinely and welcomely followed our lessons. She was an independent woman, with a lot of savvy, but later she got confused and had to go into a home, quite a nice one happily, but she didn't know me when I went to see her and was only really concerned about the sorry state of a breadfruit tree she thought she could see from her window.

I was doing an episode of "Boon", playing one of my housekeepers but this time with fangs for a nightmare scene, when the make-up artist turned out to be a Scuba instructor. I'd done a few dives in Barbados but hadn't ever got my certificate, but now her glowing accounts of the glories of the Red Sea and Indian Ocean were so exciting that I rushed off to my nearest PADI centre. This was in Notting Hill, with a shop in front and a little back room made into a pool. Water's always been my favourite element so I was taken aback to find myself useless once I'd got the tank and all the other kit on – thrashing about with my bum in the air. However I got the hang of it by the end of the first week and then we were due for our open water course, but as the proposed venue was a disused gravel quarry in Peterborough I took myself off to Malta. The sea was very boring, no coral and only a few drab fish and flat seaweed, but the PADI centre supplied a very patient and helpful young Australian instructor. I think he saw me as a bit of a challenge, so we shared the triumph when I got my certificate the day after my 81st birthday.

I must have been doing "Boon" between "Peaks" because Carlton decided there was some publicity to be got out of this "diving grannie" and I was photographed for both Radio Times and TV Times, all kitted out, both on the surface and under the water. I remember the TV Times man didn't have a weight-belt so he lay flat on the bottom and his assistant stood on him. So that was all the hard part over and now I wanted the payoff. The Australian Barrier Reef wasn't possible, alas, but diving circles said the second best reef in the world was off Belize, so I set off there, accompanied by Francine Morgan, my actress friend and tenant who's usually up for most things. After a long and exhausting journey we landed up on a very small island a few miles off the mainland. The Hotel Paradiso turned out to be a compound of little huts, with pallet beds and a solitary nail on the wall by way of wardrobe, but the island was refreshingly untouristy, with washing-lines in the yards and people going about their business, ignoring us except for an occasional not too aggressive "Hello Yankee" or, when they heard our accents, "Fuck the Queen."

I duly reported to the diving school – Fran was waiting to see how I got on first – with my certificate and diving log and was soon off to sea with three others and the diving master. He may have been nervous with this octogenarian because he wouldn't let me do the standard backflip into the water but insisted I went down the rusty ladder. Naturally it twisted and cut my leg, the usual one, but as it didn't hurt too much we went ahead with the dive. But when we all came out for the obligatory rest between dives I flooded the boat with blood and, amid dark mutters about sharks, wasn't allowed back. There was no first aid so I sat clutching the cut until the others had done their second dive and we could get back to land. Belize used to be British Honduras so it has an NHS. On the island this took the form of a twice-weekly visit by a nurse. It was one of her days – well you've got to have *some* luck – so she stitched me up and sent me off with a "There you go, just keep it dry for a week." There was nothing to do on the island but sit in the sun, eat lobster tails and get sozzled, so we took the smallest plane in the world and went to see the remains of the Mayan civilisation in Guatemala. Impressive, and we learnt quite a lot about it as our guides had their information spiel off pat, though without another word of English between them. Tiring, though, so we spent our last day drinking pina coladas in a hotel pool, Fran having agreed with me that chlorinated water couldn't hurt. Back on our island we got a better hut with a shower that worked occasionally and a wardrobe that collapsed if you hung anything in it. On a trip to another island (why didn't Fran come? Oh yes, she's nervous of boats though an excellent swimmer) I met a poet and creative writing lecturer from a college in Alaska and we all spent our last few days lazing about together.

He came to stay with me in London later and I took him on a culture trail to Shakespeare's Globe and a pretentious play at the National, and when I went off on a job he took himself to a Ray Cooney farce. Still trying to show him England, I hauled him off for a weekend in the country with George and Maggie, Grace's third daughter, where we watched a cricket match on the village green, drank in the local inn and walked through the bluebell woods. I don't remember him saying a single word. There was some talk of my going to Alaska to do my writer and director in residence bit in his college but nothing came of it.

As the years went on I dived in Cuba, Jamaica, the Virgin Islands, South Africa and Mexico – if you count Cancun as Mexico. I found it a fairly deadly place, fit only for conferences. Just one long thin road, with hotels and sea on one side and an alligator-filled lake on the other. Trying to take a short cut from the PADI centre to my hotel through Club Med's beach I was shouted at angrily by a guard and when I ignored him, guessing he wouldn't actually manhandle me, he tailed me all the way through their territory, daring me to lower my bum on to one of their precious loungers. The loungers in my hotel were mostly occupied by American matrons who wanted to talk about Charles and Camilla. I wonder if I'll ever get to the Barrier Reef. An Australian tour would be nice.

It was probably back in the sixties, perhaps between the Bangor seasons, that I wrote my only radio play to get a production. The

BBC set up a rather odd competition, requiring entrants to be sponsored by an established worker in the medium, and I was lucky enough to be sponsored by one of the best radio directors. My play didn't win but they said they'd like to do it and I was delighted when my sponsor said she'd direct it. The main character was a middle-aged blind woman and I knew a bit about the blind world because Grace's daughter Steph, whom I've mentioned once or twice, was registered blind. So I knew that blind people were much like anyone else, and certainly not pathetic. I don't know what the studios at Broadcasting House are like these days as they're said to have priced themselves out of the market so that one works in other studios, or, very comfortably, in private houses. Then, they had a glass wall between the actors and the rest of the world. The director had a mike of course, and access through the glass wall, but I sat there, helpless, while they got it basically wrong. The part was very well played but as a gentle, kindly, rather wistful soul. They'd have discussions about the character and even the meaning of lines without a glance in my direction. At one point I got frantic and grabbed a mike to explain, "It's a joke!" Puzzled, they looked at each other, then "It's a very sophisticated joke." "She's a very sophisticated woman!" Then, when the script was found to be overlong, the director sat right beside me, slashing away without a word or look at me, so at lunchtime on the second day I quietly faded away. After the transmission the director politely wrote saying she hoped I'd been happy with it and I wrote back saying no, which perhaps explains why my next radio script didn't get taken up. I was justified though by a couple of Steph's friends who rang to say well done but that wasn't the way they wanted to be seen, far too sweet. Steph died last year, in her sixties, having lived above me, next to Fran, for forty years. She was very bright, doing the most baffling logic puzzles and earning her living as a computer programmer. Maggie gave her a great funeral, with a tape of her singing with Camden Choir.

Sadly, Clem didn't live to see the end of the War. I hadn't seen her since she and Grace unexpectedly came to see me in Oldham.

Had I invited them? It seems unlikely, not that I wasn't glad to see them but I didn't expect the family to take much interest in my career, and Oldham was no holiday resort. Anyway they came for a couple of days and afterwards Clem wrote me a most generous letter, saying her talent was nothing compared to mine. She'd said, on that visit, that she'd developed diabetes and was supposed to be on a diet, but she didn't make anything of it, so it was a shock when they rang a few months later to say she'd died in a coma. I was in London but due to rehearse in Devon the next day, and they were in Buckinghamshire, so I only had time for one rushed visit, and couldn't go to the funeral. She was a cheerful, soft-hearted, life-loving person, and if she wasn't the maternal type why should she be? I once innocently asked her, when I was a kid, if she'd wanted me to be a boy or a girl before I was born and she said quite honestly that she hadn't wanted me at all and nobody wanted any more kids after the first. And then, poor woman, she got four in six years. Her sister, a born mother, never had any kids. Sod's law.

That was Auntie Ethel Smith, to distinguish her from Auntie Ethel Lewis, Dad's viper of a sister. A.E.S. was always happy to have us to stay with her and Uncle Don in the holidays. He worked for Vickers and they lived on the Vickers estate in Byfleet, a vast spread of identical houses, where everyone knew everyone's business – and salary. "Mean bugger! Drawing Office and can't stand a round!" Vickers was a bit stingy too. The rent included electricity but this was turned off in daylight in case anyone used it for electric irons. Uncle was a bit inclined to the crafty grope – "Just a bit of fun, don't tell your aunt" – but Auntie was lovely, always ready to join you in a swim in the river and even let you ride her bike, and of course it was in the country. I had some lovely times there. Poor Auntie, she didn't have the life she deserved. She hadn't been all that keen on Don but she'd been pushing thirty and there was no-one else on the horizon (this according to Clem) so she made the best of it and she really took to living in the country. Then he died in his fifties – heart attack on the bowling green – and she went back to Hackney to take care of Grandma, in the house where she'd been born. After Grandma died and Auntie was still living there I used to go over every Tuesday. There was always tinned salmon or crab, and seedcake because it was my favourite, then we'd watch telly, always "Coronation Street" and then whatever I fancied. I remember during an arts programme, as the camera panned down over Michelangelo's David's body, Auntie let out an indignant "Ooh! Rude!" Audrey Laurence, widow of the "Chinese Mandarin", lived upstairs, but she, like Auntie, was crippled with arthritis so it was fortunate that it was the East End and there were helpful neighbours, especially the people opposite, salt of the earth though with an unfortunate hatred of Jews, blacks and for some reason Italians. They kept an eye on Auntie and would ring if she was in trouble. Eventually she was. Her arthritis made it impossible for her to manage, so she went first into Hackney General and then into a series of homes, and since the family was in Kent I had to sort these out. It was difficult finding a good one, and quite a painful process, ferrying Auntie, distressed but resolutely cheerful, from place to place. I used to take a ready-mixed bottle of whiskey and water in the car so she could have a fortifying swig from time to time. She wouldn't take it into the homes though in case they found it and thought she was a drunk. At last we found a very pleasant one and she settled there quite well, though there was one decidedly unsettling incident when I was visiting and her roommate quietly died. After the first shock, Auntie and I got nervous giggles, but when I had to inform the authorities they got very official and bundled me off the premises. I suppose it was an embarrassment to have a witness to a resident's unattended death, but it seemed to me that she'd made quite an enviable exit. That was the place where the residents decided to vote which telly programmes they would watch, and when they couldn't agree, voted that the fairest thing was to show half of each programme. Kate had Auntie to live with her for a while but there really wasn't room, so she eventually lived out her life in a home near Grace, where Grace's mother-in-law, Nan, was also installed. Auntie complained that Nan pinched her fags.

Auntie Ethel Lewis was a very different kettle of fish. She was known by the family, and not with any affection, as the "Old Girl". Carneying, wheedling, evil-tongued, she'd married a rather simple man who was a talented painter but not much of a wage-earner and she made his life a misery, chucking him out of the house, and then refusing to feed him or speak to him when he crept back. She did her best to queer her daughters' pitches with their boyfriends and then had a good stab at wrecking their marriages. Finally she went from hospital to hospital and her daughters would get frantic messages, "Could you come and talk to your mother? She's bitten the nurse again." Eventually the matter seems to have been settled internally because the last message was "I'm sorry to have to tell you that Mrs. Lewis has passed away. She didn't regain consciousness after an injection."

Her daughter, Peg, is the last in our family still challenging me in the alive and kicking stakes. I told her and everyone else at my birthday party that I'd see them all in ten years' time, but I suppose there's a danger they might not all make it. Told to make a wish as I cut the cake, I heard myself shouting without a moment's hesitation, "A job! A whopping great part in a long-running series!" Seems like I'll never be cured.

Printed in the United Kingdom
by Lightning Source UK Ltd.
107295UKS00001BB/61-87